praise for

THE THROUGH LINE
and
SARA FAY EGAN

This book is both inspiring and laugh-out-loud funny! I want to be the executive producer when it becomes a movie!

—ELI MANNING

former New York Giants quarterback and Super Bowl MVP, former groom

Sara Fay's stories in *The Through Line* evoke the movie *Steel Magnolias*: her authentic voice through her storytelling conveys her resilience, thoughtfulness, and fierceness. These stories (and they are so wild, you can't make them up) demonstrate her strength, but more importantly the insight she has gained, which she generously passes on to her readers. Thank you, Sara Fay, for your honesty in storytelling and your bravery in life.

—MANDY GINSBERG

former Match Group CEO, Uber and Universal Music Group board member

The Through Line puts on display the kind of wisdom, strength, and hope we can find when we live with our eyes, hearts, and minds open. Sara Fay's honest, heartfelt storytelling invites us into her life and leaves an indelible impact on ours.

—REV. MATT TUGGLE

executive minister, Highland Park United Methodist Church

The Through Line by Sara Fay is an inspiring and actionable guide to navigating life's curveballs with grace and authenticity. Through heartfelt, hilarious, and sometimes heartbreaking real-life stories, Sara Fay shares the wisdom she's gained from overcoming life's challenges—showing us how to pursue our passions, find true contentment, and maintain meaningful relationships. This book is a must-read for anyone seeking to thrive in work, family, and life while staying true to who they are!

—LIZZIE MEANS DUPLANTIS

owner and founder of Miron Crosby, former bride

Sara Fay Egan embodies leadership with grace, passion, and perfect timing. This book is an essential read for anyone seeking to navigate the seasons of business with clarity and strength. It offers eye-opening insights, igniting a competitive spirit, a passion for excellence, and the leadership-energy needed for success. Engaging and full of common sense, it strikes the perfect balance of inspiration and practicality. I have long admired Sara Fay's kindness, passion, and ability to lead with both heart and precision. This book is a must-read for every aspiring leader.

—NARDOS IMAM

fashion designer and founder of NARDOS Design

Sara Fay masterfully walks us through her life's work, the pitfalls and personal valleys that knocked her off course but ultimately created a more fulfilled, present leader, mother, and human. *The Through Line* provides key takeaways for anyone who craves success and joy simultaneously and is chasing life's Holy Grail: balance.

—MEREDITH LAND
NBC (Dallas) anchor

Sara Fay Egan is a beacon of positivity and joy in the face of hardships. If you are looking for inspiration for your own journey through life, you need this book! Its pages contain instantly actionable insights. Sara Fay will help you see what really matters as a road map to a full life that is also fulfilling.

—LIZ BANFIELD
named top photographer by Martha Stewart Weddings, Harper's BAZAAR, *and* Brides

Sara Fay Egan's *The Through Line* is a powerful testament to passion, perseverance, and positivity. Her authenticity and vibrant personality shine through, illuminating the path she's taken to achieve remarkable heights in her career. Sara Fay's burning heart for entrepreneurship and genuine love for life and people are palpable in every page. As a bride from one of the tornado stories in this book, I can attest to her calm, unwavering strength in the midst of chaos. She gracefully rebuilt our shattered glass structures, never dimming the light during my wedding weekend. Her journey is a true inspiration.

—TREASURE MADDOX HANNAH
global fashion publicist, former bride

Sara Fay leads with vulnerability, love, and strength as she navigates life's ups and downs. This book is a testament not only to Sara Fay's leadership but is an inspiration to us all. As a career woman, a daughter, and a mother, she gives hope and perspective—and reminds us, we can have it all with faith, love, strength, and grace. This book is for anyone who has stepped back and asked, "Why?" Sara Fay has beautifully inspired us with her stories of joy, heartbreak, and happiness and reminded us we are not alone on this journey of life.

—CAPERA RYAN
mother, daughter, and deputy chairman of Christie's

the
THROUGH
line

SARA FAY EGAN

the THROUGH *line*

FINDING HAPPINESS THROUGH THE CURVEBALLS OF LIFE, FAMILY, AND BUSINESS

Copyright © 2025 by Sara Fay Egan.

All rights reserved. No part of this book may be used or reproduced in any manner whatsoever without prior written consent of the author, except as provided by the United States of America copyright law.

Published by Advantage Books, Charleston, South Carolina.
An imprint of Advantage Media.

ADVANTAGE is a registered trademark, and the Advantage colophon is a trademark of Advantage Media Group, Inc.

Printed in the United States of America.

10 9 8 7 6 5 4 3 2 1

ISBN: 979-8-89188-009-2 (Paperback)
ISBN: 979-8-89188-010-8 (eBook)

Library of Congress Control Number: 2024926447

Cover design by Analisa Smith.
Layout design by Matthew Morse.

This publication is designed to provide accurate and authoritative information in regard to the subject matter covered. It is sold with the understanding that the publisher is not engaged in rendering legal, accounting, or other professional services. If legal advice or other expert assistance is required, the services of a competent professional person should be sought.

> Advantage Books is an imprint of Advantage Media Group. Advantage Media helps busy entrepreneurs, CEOs, and leaders write and publish a book to grow their business and become the authority in their field. Advantage authors comprise an exclusive community of industry professionals, idea-makers, and thought leaders. For more information go to **advantagemedia.com**.

This book is dedicated to my loving husband, Merrick,
who is my rock and my best friend.

To my beautiful daughter, Grace:
I cannot wait to watch you grow and flourish in life.
I am so proud of you.

To my sweet son, Walker:
your kindness and love for others will take you so far in life.

To my mother, Joan, and my sister, Grace,
who have stood by my side through it all: I love you.

You are my everything.

CONTENTS

Acknowledgments xv

Preface xvii

Introduction
Joy as a Guiding Principle for Success 1

Chapter One
Embracing Authenticity 7
    Next Up, CNN 11
    Forging Ahead 11
    All In 14
    Reflections from My Early Working Days 15
    Leaping into the Unknown 17
    The End Goal Is the Same 20
    Perfection versus Authenticity 22
    If the Kitchen Is On Fire, Keep Smiling! 23
    Chapter One Takeaways and Reflections 27

Chapter Two
Shifting Gears to Overcome Challenges 31
    The God Moments 38
    Counting Our Blessings and Adapting to the New Normal ... 40
    But This Can't Happen to Me 42

    Shifting Gears When You Cannot Control the People around You 46
    Customs Nightmare 49
    Events to Restaurant Management Overnight 51
    Chapter Two Takeaways and Reflections 61

Chapter Three

Cultivating Human Connection 67

    Out of Office 69
    You Wouldn't Believe 72
    The Business of Being Yourself Helps You to Connect................... 73
    Chameleon Sales 75
    Eye Contact 76
    It's the People! 76
    Making a Getaway 79
    Chapter Three Takeaways and Reflections 81

Chapter Four

Whenever Possible, Have a Backup Plan 85

    My Support System.. 88
    One for the Books—or in This Case, My Book! 90
    When You Don't Have a Backup Plan 95
    Interviewing Clients, Potential Employees, and Friends 98
    A Sad Backup Plan.. 100
    Getting Caught Off Guard 102
    Chapter Four Takeaways and Reflections 104

Chapter Five

Leading with Focus................................... 107

    The Boss's Daughter 109
    How to Build a Road Map to Lead Effectively 110
    Chapter Five Takeaways and Reflections............................... 123

Chapter Six

Balancing Personal and Professional Life **125**

    Work Hard, Play Hard 127

    The Mom Guilt Is Real! 128

    When I Finally Got It 130

    The Struggle Is Real....................................... 131

    The Final Straw.. 133

    Chapter Six Takeaways and Reflections................. 135

Chapter Seven

Preserving Our Families, Culture, History, and Businesses . 139

    Passing It Down... 141

    What Makes You Special? 142

    What Made Our Family Special?......................... 144

    Preserving What Matters.................................. 146

    Chapter Seven Takeaways and Reflections 147

Chapter Eight

Right Here Is Perfect **149**

    Being in the Present 153

    Is the Grass Always Greener?............................. 154

    Chapter Eight Takeaways and Reflections 156

Conclusion

When You Get Down, Get Back Up! **159**

Let's Connect!.. **161**

About the Author **165**

ACKNOWLEDGMENTS

To Patricia, my mother-in law, and Emily, my sister-in-law, but they are actually a sister and mother to me. I love you deeply, and my favorite life memories are with you.

To my stepfather, Mike Heflin, who stepped up and helped us in ways that were unimaginable and always handled every decision with utmost integrity. Mike, I look up to you like a true father.

To my confidant, mentor, and constant cheerleader Jacquelin Sewell Atkinson.

To my first boss, Todd Fiscus, who taught me so much about business and event planning.

To my Beale Street Blues Company corporate team, Todd Becker, Kim Coen, Larry O'Connor, and Oscar Pena.

To my cheerleaders, Jessica, Allie, Meredith, Wynne, and Katy. Thank you for loving me and supporting me always.

To my close friends, you know who you are, my tribe.

To our Dallas family, Peggy and Carl Sewell.

To my attorney, Neal Graham, don't worry ... I didn't even tell half of it!

To Dr. Benjamin Greenberg, Grace's neurologist at UT Southwestern Medical Center, Dallas.

To Candice Judd, our elementary school principal. Without you, our family would not be where we are today.

To my doctor, Dr. Eugene Hunt, thank you for praying with me during the hardest times.

To Matt Tuggle who continuously inspires me to be a better person.

To Suzanna de Boer who has been my sounding board while writing this book.

To Liz Banfield, Lizzie Duplantis, Mandy Ginsberg, Treasure Maddox Hannah, Nardos Imam, Meredith Land, Eli Manning, and Capera Ryan for writing the most heartfelt testimonials.

PREFACE

My name is Sara Fay Egan, and I live in Dallas, Texas, with my husband, Merrick, my thirteen-year-old daughter, Grace, and my ten-year-old son, Walker. Boy, do I have stories. I have been through so much the past few years and have come out on the other side feeling happier and healthier. I have been taken out of my comfort zone and put in situations I never thought I would be put in. I have ended up in places I never thought my life would take me and which were not part of my perfect plan. But somehow, along the way, I have found happiness—a true sense of fulfillment and satisfaction. I wanted to write this book for you if you are in the middle of something right now, or maybe you just want to be prepared for what life throws at you in the future. I do not want anyone to have to go through some of the things I've been through. Just take it from me so you do not have to live it and learn firsthand. I want the stories in this book to inspire you. All of the stories are based on my own life, whether with my family or in my event-planning work. Hopefully you will be inspired to make changes in your own life while being greatly entertained at the same time!

I went to the University of Mississippi for college and met my husband while studying abroad in Innsbruck, Austria, in my junior year. We moved to Dallas after college, and I began working for Todd Events as an event planner. After eight years there, I was pregnant with

Grace and decided that I needed a change. I was always on a plane, and work was my first and foremost priority. I had already missed so many family experiences, friends' weddings, and time with my husband. I did not feel like I was a good wife, friend, daughter, or sister, and I did not want to be that kind of mother.

Why could I not do both—be a mother and have a successful career? I believed I could. So, I decided to do things my way instead, and I started my own event design company called Jackson Durham Floral and Event Design with my business partner, Heath Alan Ray. While starting a new business and having a baby sounded like it would be easier than working for someone else, I found out otherwise, and I learned a lot of lessons along that journey. I went on to sell that business six years later and carried on with a new business I called Sara Fay Egan Events, which specialized in planning weddings and events around the world, including Italy, Mexico, Jamaica, the Bahamas, Colorado, California, Maine, Texas, Tennessee, Mississippi, Louisiana, Wyoming, New York, North Carolina, Florida, South Carolina, Wisconsin, Rhode Island, and Oklahoma to name a few!

It was my passion for sure. I loved each and every detail of every event, but most of all, I loved the people. I loved the vendors who were like family to me: Alyssa, who did our graphic design; Mike, who constructed our tents; Nelson, who was a design genius, transforming temporary spaces into permanent structures; Joe, who would do anything to get power to our clients across the country; and Matt and his team, who risked electrocution in thunderstorms to put together our lighting design. They were the ones that made it all happen. Not to mention how I felt about my clients! While some were difficult, they challenged me to work even harder to make them happy. I am a people pleaser at heart, and it was very important to always make my clients happy. I was working with families at such a special and important time in their life. Tensions were high, expectations were high, and the chance of something going wrong was high. But I loved it. I loved the drama, I loved the adrenaline, and I loved the excitement. Nothing made me happier than walking through a field in rain boots, creating a tent that looked like a permanent structure and detailed to the client's personality and dreams. It was my greatest joy.

However, in September of 2021, my father passed away suddenly of COVID, and my life changed overnight.

Suddenly, I was president of his restaurant group, Beale Street Blues Company. My entire life was flipped upside down. I was planning weddings around the world and running restaurants at the same time. My phone never stopped ringing. I was thrown into managing a team as the "boss's daughter," which is a hard position to be in when you are used to being respected in your career. Then, in November of 2021, my daughter suddenly became very sick with autoimmune encephalitis to the point where some days she could not walk or talk. My entire world changed again and came to a complete halt as we navigated forty nights in the hospital.

My entire life, people have told me, "You should write a book!" Looking back at all my experiences, I see a through line. I see how it all connects, and I would love to tell my stories in a way that helps you navigate the storms with positivity and joy—to come out on the other side and think about what you appreciate. I would love for you to not have to go through the storms I have been through to learn the lessons. Just take it from me.

I am originally from Memphis, Tennessee. I loved growing up in Memphis. I knew it was a special place when I was growing up there. I loved the feel of the South. I loved the food, the music, the weather, the accents, the Southern hospitality. I had an appreciation for where I was from at a young age. But I always knew I wanted more. I knew

the THROUGH *line*

there was a much bigger world out there that I needed to explore, people I needed to meet.

I went to Hutchison School, which is an all-girls school, with the same sixty girls in my grade from kindergarten to twelfth grade. The school instilled in me from a young age that I could do anything I put my mind to, and I truly believed it. I was very naive and thought I would move to New York City for a year, Washington, DC, for a year, then on to Paris and London. Whatever my future was, I knew it was not in Memphis. I appreciated where I came from but wanted more. Life has a funny way of directing you to places you never thought you would go, but somehow, it ends up being messy and perfect all at the same time. I am forty-two now and have finally learned to enjoy the ride. I have so many stories along the way of how I have gotten to the point I'm at today.

I have learned so many lessons, and I often think to myself, I wish I'd known that before. I wish someone had told me that. I believe in mentoring. I would love to pass along any wisdom I have learned whether from my wedding and event planning experiences or from my experiences running the restaurant group. Most of the stories are hard to believe! I laugh that the movie *The Wedding Planner* was a great love story, but it could have been a lot funnier with real crazy stories. My personal experiences have been wonderful, life-altering, sad, and joyful.

I believe it is how we tie all these experiences together and learn from them that matters. I have tried to do work and family life well and failed many times along the way. I have learned that the people at the end of the day are really all that matters, the people right in front of you—you just have to open your eyes to see what's already right there. We will laugh a lot, we will cry a little, and in the end, I hope you will leave with a joyful outlook on your career, your family, and your friends. Life is what we make it. You have the keys.

This idea, I like to call the through line—connecting the dots through all of your life experiences together to give you purpose and a happy and fulfilled life.

What is your through line? Is it your values? Is it your experiences? What details of your story can you weave together to make sense of it all? What do you have that makes you special? Use it!

Is this book for you? This book is for anyone that is seeking to have a well-rounded life. Maybe you have not had a lot of business or life experience yet. I don't want you to have to learn the hard way! Learn from me. This book is for the person that believes they can have it all: family, friends, and a career. I'm here to say, do it! You can do it all and be happy!

If you want to take what you have that's special and turn it into something but also live a fulfilled and happy life … then this is the book for you.

Introduction

JOY AS A GUIDING PRINCIPLE FOR SUCCESS

On paper, it looks like I've had it all in my life: celebrity weddings, dream projects, high-end clients—all of the exciting stories that I used to call home to tell my mom about. They sound sexy and glamorous, but I have realized those stories are just stories. They are not the ones that fill my cup, fill my soul, or really leave me with anything at the end of the day. I have spent years and years on the hamster wheel, chasing the next client, the next project, the next dream. The funny thing is that my team and I spend hours and hours planning the perfect wedding in Italy or Mexico in the most ideal setting, but after the ceremony and celebration, the details that were once important become a thing of the past. Most of the beautiful decorations that everyone admired are thrown in the trash. The wedding is suddenly torn down, and the client that called me ten times a day doesn't need me anymore.

It is somewhat of a lonely feeling. Have you ever felt that way? You're living through a time where your Instagram feed shows that you are on top of the world, or you tell your friends a story and they seem jealous of what is happening in your life. But maybe on the inside, you still feel a little empty. Like, what is wrong with me? This is a huge thing! This is what I wanted! Why am I not happy?

But I would contrast it with another experience to show perspective. For example, recently I was walking through Target with my daughter Grace and my son Walker. This may not seem special and may seem like an everyday activity that you may even take for granted. But I was always too busy for moments like this. I would use Amazon for what I needed or had a sitter take the kids to shop. That's because I was always trying to maximize my time to do the most and multitask. Does that sound familiar to you too?

On this day, Grace, Walker, and I were just walking down the aisles. Not in a rush, not in a hurry, just being silly and present. We were aimlessly wandering through the outdoor pool toy aisle and remembering the time last summer when we'd had the water balloon fight ... and the time during the COVID lockdown when we had put all the cheesy blow-up pool toys and slides together to make a fort. We laughed and smiled, and I thought to myself in the moment, *My heart is so full.* Staring at the red cart, completely lost in my thoughts, I suddenly had a profound sense of happiness and fulfillment. How in the world could I be so happy walking through an aisle of Target? They tell you this time goes by so fast. Why had I been going so fast? Could we just press the pause button? Have you felt that way before? Have you heard the saying with kids that "the days are long and the years are short"? I feel like we know this. Why can't we learn from it and do better?

I remember during the first part of the COVID lockdown being scared but happy at the same time, feeling like my May schedule was so jam-packed with events that I actually did not know how I was going to get through those days. Then poof, my schedule was cleared. I felt guilty for feeling a sense of relief when so many people were sick and dying. I remember thinking to myself that something was wrong with the way I was living life if it took a pandemic to slow me down. Why could I not say no before? Why did I feel like I had to pack my schedule with work, school activities, kids' schedules, and social events? Who was this for? Was it for me? I was stressed. Was it for my kids? They were stressed. Our family was actually out of whack completely. So why were we on the hamster wheel? Do you ever feel like you are on the hamster wheel and don't know how to get off?

After everything that life had thrown at me, I did not take lightly the importance of this moment in Target. I reflected that what the world views as success and as accomplishments did not align with what my heart felt were success and accomplishments anymore. I think that is why successful people are always searching, whether it is searching for God, another project, another house, another client, another exercise routine. How can we be successful and enjoy that moment at the same time? We are always trying to figure that out, especially under the high pressures and stress that success requires.

Do not get me wrong, I still want it all. Does this sound like you too? My all is just different now. My all looks less like the perfect job in New York and more about being present in the moments with both my family and my work.

My life has been exciting to say the least. I have had the highest of highs and the lowest of lows. As I have gotten older, I have realized the importance of how these times and stories and people have shaped my life, where I am today, and, especially, who I am today. This book is meant to help readers find and embrace joy as a guiding principle for success in the face of life's challenges, including working in a demanding industry, managing high-stress situations, and navigating the ever-changing landscape of the "experience" economy, on top of being a spouse, parent, caretaker, and community leader.

So, what's the purpose of this book, Sara Fay?

The purpose of this book is … to guide you through your own journey. I will take you on a journey through my personal and professional experiences in the events industry as well as the food and beverage industry. I have found throughout all these experiences that I have learned to focus on embracing authenticity, overcoming challenges, cultivating human connection, and finding a balance between personal and professional life. And I hope my insights will help you to find that balance too.

As I mentioned earlier, during my whole career, I have been trying to tie each day together with what I call a through line. It has hit me that during the past few years, I am now trying to tie my whole life together as a through line. How do I make sense of all these experiences that have happened to me—the good, the bad, the sad, the ugly—and eventually someday leave this life feeling like it was meaningful?

This concept on a surface level can be applied to almost anything in life. For me, in the event industry, I have been explaining this concept to clients for over twenty years.

Think about it … you get engaged! Wow! The moment you have been waiting for. It feels like everyone you have run into for months (and maybe years) has asked if your partner is the one and if you will get married. While all these people mean well, they are creating this underlying pressure on you to create the "perfect moment," the "perfect event," the "perfect life." Even the most reasonable and down-to-earth person gets tied up in the crazy during wedding planning, the quest to make it the best, the thing that no one has seen before.

As a bride, one of the first things you do is send out a "save the date" for the wedding day. But that is so much pressure! You think to yourself, What is my theme? Do I need a monogram? What are my colors? Suddenly you have all this pressure on yourself to come up with the perfect thing. And it's like you can't come up with that perfect thing right that moment out of thin air when you don't know the ending! You don't know all the details of the wedding. How can you set the tone when you haven't planned the rest?

Life is like this. How can you make huge, life-changing decisions each day that affect the trajectory of your life without knowing the end? One decision can completely change things. It is a lot of pressure for anyone! I personally want this book to help you take the experiences you have faced in life and connect the dots. How do they all tie together for you? I want to help you to not put so much pressure on yourself and enjoy the ride, the small moments. You will make a wrong turn, a bad decision. But how can you learn from this and make this part of your whole through line of life?

If you are single and cannot relate to the wedding day, you certainly can relate to college and graduating from college. What is the perfect thing for you, the perfect internship, the perfect job, the perfect city? What if you choose wrong? That can be very anxiety-building and a stressful way to live, especially when comparing ourselves to others, which only leaves us feeling empty and depressed. Whereas when you look at it from a through-line perspective, for me, you say, OK, yes, I have an entire wedding to plan with ten thousand details. But the "save the date" is just a piece of telling this story. There are lots of stationery pieces for the entire wedding. You have the invitation, the weekend guide, the program—all these other pieces. If you change your mind later on with colors or the theme, that is fine! The "save the date" can be a one-off fun thing! It is just a date; it is just paper; it does not define you! However, the wedding does.

My hope is that after reading this book, you will learn to build meaningful relationships with your own customers and clients, leading to improved service, customer loyalty, and personal fulfillment and that you will walk away with valuable insights, actionable strategies, and relatable, "crazy" stories you can see yourself in. I hope that from the stories on these pages, you learn to infuse joy into every interaction, creating memorable experiences that bring happiness to both customers and service providers as well as to your own life. I also hope that you can learn from my lessons and hard work to get to where you want to be faster.

No matter how bleak your life or situation might become, I want you to know you can handle it and even enjoy the moments along the way. Take it a day at a time. I told my son the other day when he was upset about his football game, "Just smile; seriously, smile really big right now." He did it against his wishes, then he suddenly burst out laughing. I said, "See, it is impossible to be mad when your face is smiling."

Through the pages of this book, let's find your through line together, a through line for happiness, friendship, work, and life. It is OK to shift gears, but let's take these experiences and tie them together to make the most of any moment, enjoy the small things, look people in the eye, and laugh a lot. That is what life is all about.

It just takes one person. And that person is you. How can you make a difference with your own life, your own family, your own friends, your own career? I promise you can.

Chapter One

EMBRACING AUTHENTICITY

Leaping into the Unknown

Being a star just means that you find your own special place, that you shine where you are.

—DOLLY PARTON

The dream, according to my twenty-one-year-old self:

My makeup was perfect, my hair was curled. I put on my white button-down shirt and black Ann Taylor blazer. From the waist up, I was oozing professionalism. I stopped there. I threw on red Soffe gym shorts and flip flops and ran out the door of the sorority house to the Journalism building next door. I was running a little late that day and needed time to read through the teleprompter for the 5:00 p.m. student newscast. Well, it did not matter that I was a few minutes late, because the teleprompter was broken. I do not like not being prepared. I had to read through the news stories before I went on air. What if I stumbled over the words? What if I mispronounced something? What if I looked stupid? I said to myself, *Fake it till you make it, Sara Fay. You always have, so don't stop now.* Plus, who was watching? Maybe my grandfather a few counties away, and definitely my journalism professor. There was a good chance no one else. It's fine; just take a deep breath and be yourself.

The teleprompter started working at 4:59 p.m. Perfect; we could go on-air. I just had no idea what the stories were. That is OK … just smile. It was just like cheerleading, except I couldn't mouth "W-A-T-E-R-M-E-L-O-N" if I did not know the words. Shoot, here goes. The first block went well. I had Don sitting next to me, and he would definitely not make any mistakes. I could tell he watched CNN for fun just to pick up on the transition words, and he always perfectly ended the A block with "rather" or other perfect words he could muster up. *Shoot*, I thought to myself, *I need to do that. Note to self: make a list of transition words.*

I love making lists. I love making lists almost as much as I love crossing things off my list. *Add to list: forget watching CNN, apply for internship at CNN!* My mind was spinning, but my daydreaming had to wait, as I saw the director raise his hand and signal to me. *Great!* I thought to myself. It looked like a fluffy C block story about cats. *I can do this!* I began in my best professional news anchor voice, "The Oxford humane society is hosting a fundraiser to adopt a litter of kittens." The B-roll scrolled images of cute kittens. Oh good, animals were always a slam dunk when it came to news stories! Nothing could go wrong here. I smiled the biggest cheerleader smile I could muster up as the adorable animals faded, and the camera cut to me. My face was still locked in that smile as the next story scrolled. "President Bush announced today that bio—"… *Shoot, I am about to say "bioterrorism." How do I switch my tone quickly from cheerleader to Barbara Walters?* I gave myself the biggest internal pep talk and yelled to myself, *Just do it, Sara Fay; you cannot smile and say the word "terrorism"!* "Bio" came out with the *huge* smile, and I abruptly frowned to say "terrorism" in the deepest, most serious voice I could muster. *Shoot, that wasn't me doing a Barbara Walters vocal style; that was more like Tom Brokaw. I sounded like I was speaking with a seventy-year-old man's deep voice!*

How do I recover? Oh no, here she comes. My internal pep talk kicked in again in an even more serious tone. *Push her back; don't let her come out!* The *real* Sara Fay was *way* too fun for the Barbara Walters vocal style. But it was too late; a full-on laughing attack had hit me. As much as I tried to push it down, the laughter would not stop. The producers were staring at me with their eyes, saying, "What is funny about terrorism?" This wasn't part of the plan. *Stop laughing, Sara Fay,* I told myself. *How are you going to be on the* Today Show *if you can't get a sentence out with two viewers watching? Goodness gracious,* the narrative in my head rolled along. They cut to commercial, and Don took the next story. Don would *never* have a laughing attack. He was as serious as serious could get. He was no fun at a party! *Well,* I thought, *I would rather be with me at a party. Oh well.* But deep down, the laughter filled up my heart a little bit more than being the serious person I was "supposed" to be. Was I cut out for this world? But I couldn't pivot now!

Authentic Lessons Learned

Maybe I didn't need to be reading someone else's lines. Maybe I needed to be doing something where my personality could shine through more and I could be myself.

- Is your personality able to shine through in your day-to-day role?

  _____

  _____

- Are the people you surround yourself with supportive of who you really are? Or are they trying to shape you into something else?

  _____

  _____

  - Coworkers: _____
  - Friends: _____
  - Family: _____

- Is there something else you should be doing to let your inner light shine brighter?

  _____

  _____

Next Up, CNN

My résumé was going to be *amazing*! The internship did not pay, and I had to wear pantyhose in July, but let's not get caught up in the details. This was the big leagues. Welcome to CNN; here is your closet for the next two months to sit in with no windows. The director of public relations said, "This is a box of VHS tapes. Can you play these on the VHS player? It is footage of the war in Iraq, and I need you to write down the time down to the second where the reporter says the word *America*." What? I am supposed to go sit in a closet and do what? Well, at least my mom still had bragging rights about the big leagues. No one had to know I was in a dark closet with itchy pantyhose. But this is what I was "supposed" to do. What about the *Today Show*? How was I going to get there from this closet? This really was not fun. I felt lonely. My boyfriend of one year, Merrick, was forty-five minutes away from Atlanta in Athens, Georgia, for the summer. That sounded way more fun than being trapped here. But I had to keep my head in the game. I started driving to Athens more and more to fill up my cup. I couldn't tell anyone at work I had a boyfriend. You do not make it to the top by being distracted by a boy. What about New York? I had dreams.

Forging Ahead

I sent my résumé tape to every state and a few islands. Surely, I would get a few callbacks. Maybe in a year, I would be in New York. I got one callback. *One.* Tyler, Texas. Merrick had moved to Dallas, so Tyler seemed close. "Your interview is at 6:00 a.m. with the producer of the morning show at the Tyler NBC affiliate." Sounds fancy! I woke up at 3:30 a.m. and made the drive to Tyler for my 6:00 a.m. interview. Who has a 6:00 a.m. interview? I walked in and sat down in the producer's office. She got right to the point. By 6:02 a.m., she had already told me: 1) if you work here, you will have to go to speech lessons, because you have the worst accent, 2) you will have to cut your hair; it is too long, and 3) you will have to change your name. You cannot have a double name like Sara Fay on air.

OK, I thought to myself, *I guess I will turn around and drive right back. Thank you for telling me everything that is wrong with me.* But then she said, "*But* … I like the way you dress, and I like the way you write … so why don't you stick around for the day?" What? This was the weirdest way to start an interview, and it did not seem very positive at all. There was one cute girl in the newsroom that looked nice, and she was looking at eye shadow online. My kind of girl. Maybe she could be a friend. She passed her card and said, "Before you sign anything, call me!" She went on, "I really wish I could buy this Mary Kay eye shadow for $3.50, but I can't this month, and I am stuck here for three years." Maybe this wasn't for me. But this was my dream!

I went back to Dallas and had a job interview at Todd Events with Todd Fiscus. He was the premier party planner in Dallas and had just started his own company. I mean, I was social chair of my sorority. I couldn't be that hard to train. But I knew I had a lot to learn, and this was Dallas, not Oxford, Mississippi, putting together a crawfish boil in a field. I better study up!

So, I did what any self-respecting interviewee would do. I went to Barnes & Noble and bought the bright-yellow book *Wedding Planning for Dummies*. This would at least get me though the interview. I sat down at the table at the bookstore with my neon-yellow highlighter. I was going to be prepared. I studied and memorized the ways to set the dining table. I knew exactly where each fork went if I was quizzed. I had never seen so many forks in my life. I felt a little like Julia Roberts with her oyster fork. "Slippery little sucker!" I told myself, *It worked out for her! I have got this!* I drove to the interview listening to my favorite Dixie Chicks song, belting out loud, "Wide open spaces … room to make the big mistakes!"

> **PRO TIP**
>
> *Always have a female power ballad ready to play in your car; it is the perfect motivation for the day, and especially for an interview.*

I pulled up a few minutes early and studied my flash cards one more time. I walked in wearing my black pinstripe suit and black suede grommet kitten heels. I felt like a million bucks!

I was met by David at the front desk. He was perfectly dressed from head to toe in couture. I could see a black Birkin bag sitting behind him on the credenza. He was writing with a gray pen that was labeled "Prada" across the side. As I glanced up, I noticed a green Gucci faux-flower boutonniere on his lapel. I thought to myself, *I am not in Mississippi anymore, and this is* not *a field party; this is the* big *leagues!*

His smile was contagious as he said hello while I could feel him simultaneously checking me out head to toe. This was going to be fun! A much better welcome than the dark newsroom! I met with Todd for about twenty minutes. He asked me about my outfit, my shoes, my summer, my sorority. We quickly realized we were both captain of our high school cheerleading teams, both social chairmen of our fraternity and sororities, and both loved a party. We laughed, and as he wrapped up the conversation, I thought to myself that he really didn't say much about events or what exactly I would be doing, but I knew I liked him! I was going to fake it until I made it! He stood up and said, "Well, when can you start?" I looked around, waiting for the quiz on where to place the salad fork on the table. Really?

The next week, I had heard back from both job offers. I received an offer from the news station for the morning show. *My dream.* But this meant that I was going to have to live in Tyler, Texas, for at least three years, where I knew no one. I had dated Merrick for two and a half years at this point and owed it to our relationship to see if it could work in the same town. But I couldn't move somewhere for a boy. What about all that female power I was taught in school? What about *all* those things I did to make my résumé four pages long? What about my CNN internship? I could not throw that away. I decided I would give it a try. After all, it was about the people, and I liked the feeling of being in that office. I decided to try it. I thought, *I will give this event-planning thing my all, and if in a year I do not like it or my relationship doesn't work out, I can move to New York.* It's funny, but I still have the same philosophy about most things in my life, which has helped me to shift gears in both family, life, and business.

All In

If I was going to do it, then I was going to be the best. Wait, what was my title exactly? Well, whatever it was, I was going to be the best at it! I followed Todd around everywhere he went. I had a tape recorder with me and recorded our meetings. He spoke so fast and brilliantly, and I did not know what half of the terms meant. I would go back to my desk at night once it was dark and everyone had left and rewind the recorder, look up the meanings of words I didn't know, and type up the recap and proposal for him to have the next morning. I had *no* clue what I was doing. But I worked hard. I came early; I stayed late. It felt good to be part of the team.

It felt good to be creating something. It took me a few years to realize what exactly I liked about the job. I had never dreamed about being a wedding planner. But here I was, running the wedding division. I had people reporting to me, and soon, I was a vice president of the company. How did that happen? I wasn't sure. I just put my head down and worked hard. I would load the trucks with the correct inventory and double check it each time before the truck left to make sure we were prepared for each event. If there was a mess on the floor, I would grab a broom; if there was a candle that needed to be lit, I would grab a lighter. I think back to these days, and no one told me to do these things. There was a sense of team with no hierarchy. Everyone would step in and do any job at any time that needed to be done to make the event happen. I think these days truly shaped my outlook on a great work ethic.

I also truly feel that, because of those days, I was able to gain the respect of everyone on my team, from the truck driver to the floral team to the accountant to the contract worker. This mindset has stayed with me to this day and I think can be translated to any line of work and any industry.

I had no idea at the time, but these early experiences were shaping my approach to teamwork and leadership, and I attribute much of my success to it. It was the beginning lesson of a through line that I could weave throughout all aspects of my life and career.

Reflections from My Early Working Days

For the first ten years probably in the event-planning world, I lived by the motto, "Fake it until you make it." I would smile and usually say yes, then figure it out. It worked for a long time, and honestly, if you have a hard work ethic, usually it can get you through most situations.

You must realize every single person does not know everything about what they are doing.

You must be constantly learning your whole life—learning about your industry, learning new ways of doing things, growing. I truly believe the second you stop learning is the second you are finished. The best people at life are still learning. Be a sponge; soak it all up.

I have also found that authenticity is the key. Being authentic enough to admit that you do not know everything helps people to trust you, to see the real you. Authenticity helps people realize you are real, and they can work with you through this together. Even the presidents, the CEOs, and the smartest people in the room had to start somewhere.

There are so many wonderful people out there. I have always been so busy moving on to the next thing in life that I forgot to stop and look people in the eye at times and ask them how they were doing. I learned this lesson the past few years. I never had time for anyone—my family, my friends, conversations that did not lead to an immediate solution for the problem at hand. I was a doer. I was always doing, which meant I usually was going somewhere. This got me pretty far in life ... until it didn't.

Life, to me, is all about the people in it and the people you surround yourself with, both in work and in your personal life. I have learned the hard way that the older I get, the more I feel the need to keep my circle small and family close. Have you felt that way recently? I think this feeling becomes more apparent during difficult times.

Make a list right now. Write down the first five people that you would call if something significant happened in your life.

Are those the five people that you spend the most time with? Are they the people you always answer the phone for, or do you sometimes ignore their calls because you know them so well you think it's OK, and anyway, you are busy with the task at hand?

I know I am guilty of that. I heard someone say, you can have one hundred friends and be the loneliest person, but you can have five true friends and be the richest person.

Ultimately, I want to become a person who is shaped by the people in my life and a person who values the relationships in my life. My hope is that for you as well.

Reflect on your current life situations and consider whether the people you surround yourself with allow you to be authentic.

Leaping into the Unknown

My father, Tommy, was an accountant and started his own venture capital firm. He wore a suit and tie every day to work. He always looked very uncomfortable. As he would come home from work each day, he would immediately start adjusting his tie from right to left as soon as he hit the first step. The uncomfortable twitch I saw in his neck and the stress visible in his eyes made me really not want to grow up.

I remember one night clearly. It was 1993, and I was in fourth grade. I was sitting at the green kitchen island doing my homework as he approached the back doorstep that evening. Something was different about him. When his foot hit the first step, I noticed he had already removed his tie. In fact, his top button was already unbuttoned, and he was smiling ear to ear. He appeared to be happy for the first time I could remember in a while. As he came into the kitchen, he explained that some of the city leaders of Memphis and Beale Street had come to him to help revitalize Beale Street. They wanted him to open a B. B. King's Blues Club at the famous corner of Second Avenue and Beale Street. My father had always loved music. You never rode in the car with him without him playing the game "Guess who is playing guitar on this song?" He loved Crystal Gayle, Otis Redding,

Sam & Dave, Al Green, and Van Morrison, to name a few. The spark of excitement that I saw in his eye that night, I did not recognize.

In the '50s, '60s, and '70s, Memphis was overflowing with music, culture, blues, sounds, smells, foods. There was so much deep history and soul around the area and all down the Mississippi River, but Beale Street was now boarded up. The sounds that were once there had faded away, and the streets where B. B. King and Elvis once walked and strummed their guitars were empty. I had no idea that night that my father's life, my family's life, and my life would change forever.

I remember B. B. King coming to dinner. I had heard his name before, as he was often one of the answers to my father's game in the car. "Turn up the radio! Who sings this song *and* is playing guitar on this song?" He knew it all. He loved music. It was in his soul, and he always knew it could make him feel better after a long day, no matter what was happening with his deals.

I do believe everything happens for a reason, and suddenly, my father was not wearing his tie every day and was driving downtown and pouring his heart and soul into every detail of this new restaurant. He began embracing his own inner being and authentic self. Now that I reflect on his life's parallels to my life, I realize that his life previously looked good on paper just like mine had: a beautiful wife, beautiful daughters, a house, a great job. Who could ask for more? I do not think at that time he knew what was happening, but it was a slow progression toward allowing himself to follow his heart and what made him happy instead of what the world told him he should be doing and what looked good on paper.

He knew nothing about restaurants, but he had heart, soul, and love for people. I really believe if you deeply love something and give it your all, the rest will fall into place. His love was music. He knew that if the music was "just right," the sound level was "just right," and the atmosphere and food were "just right," we could catapult the guests to a different place, a place back in time to a Memphis that was no longer there anymore.

Looking back, I think he needed to be at that place. He needed to be taken back to that time. I believe he looked up one day and thought, "How did I get here? How did I end up being an accountant? Well, I am good at numbers, but this is zero creativity and zero soul. I am married to the first girl I met on the first day of college while I was at the bookstore. She is beautiful, and I do not deserve her, but am I happy? I have three beautiful daughters ... but is there more? I need another level of fulfillment."

I believe he created B. B. King's Blues Club as not only a place that he could escape to, but also that anyone could escape to. And it was one. It later became a place where the flippers on Beale Street flipping for money would come in for a burger, but also, on any given night, you might see Justin Timberlake jump onstage with the house band. Everyone felt good there. It was a feel-good place.

The road as Tommy's daughter was hard. I saw my mom at home many nights alone taking care of the kids. I felt like work meant more to him than I did at times. But looking back, I am proud of him. I am proud of him for making the decision to follow his dream, to follow his heart, follow his soul. And in the end, he ended up right where he needed to be and made a difference in people's lives along the way.

If I could give advice to him now, I would say, "It's OK to follow your dreams, love your family, be a dad, and be a husband. You can do it all. You do not have to choose one over the other." I think that is the big picture that people miss these days. They think they must either have a career or be a mom. I wholeheartedly believe you can do both and do both well. It just doesn't look like you think it should on paper. You just must make it work for your life! There are no rules!

I want my kids to know this authentic place that my father was searching for, this feeling. In a world where everything is bright and shiny and there is AI versus doing the work yourself, in this fast-paced, cutthroat world, I am happy to be doing what I am doing. I think that is what I have always loved to do, whether it was managing a wedding, an event, or now a restaurant.

The End Goal Is the Same

My goal for both events and restaurants is to have the guest come in, and they just can't quite put their finger on it. The lighting doesn't stand out because it is dimmed perfectly. The music isn't too loud or too quiet but is the perfect sound and the perfect feel-good music you need at the moment. The music is perfectly curated, a quieter dinner set of songs you find yourself singing aloud to. Then, you suddenly find yourself on the dance floor, singing at the top of your lungs, and you have no idea how you got there, and it is a Tuesday night. Then we know we did it. We did our job. Because that guest left thinking, *Tonight was perfect. Tonight was just what I needed.* Whatever is going on in that person's life—and something is going on in everyone's life—whatever it is, no matter how big or small, we were able to transport them to a different place for a few hours, a place of joy, love, warmth, and soul. All elements of the senses came together at once—smell, taste, sound, touch, and ambiance—and it was just what they needed.

The biggest compliment for me at a wedding is having the guest walk in and say, "This is *so* Caroline." That means that I did my job. Not one element stands out that I designed for the wedding, but rather that that the client's personality showed through in the details. And then the music, food, drinks, decor—nothing overpowers the other. They are all amazing in their own right, and nothing is forgotten.

For restaurants, and specifically B. B. King's and Itta Bena, others all over the world have tried to replicate the soulful culture and ambiance and food, but there is something about the true patina on Beale Street that you never can quite match.

It is funny looking back and knowing my dad's why and seeing how his why wove its way into my why. We had completely different paths, different attitudes, different states, different directions, different passions. But we both had a burning heart for entrepreneurism inside us, a love for life, and a love for people. For both of us, it is all about the people.

If your heart is with your people, whether it is your employees, your customers, your clients, or your family, you will end up on top. It may not always seem fair in the short term, as greedy people somehow seem to win the short game. But I believe that by staying the course long-term in a genuine way, doing what you know is right, and keeping your focus on the soul of the people, you will win every time.

- **Do you find yourself leading with your heart or leading with your head?**

  _____

  _____

- **Have you thought about that, and how you could change it?**

  _____

  _____

  _____

the THROUGH *line*

Perfection versus Authenticity

My husband and I were about to put our house up for sale. I told Merrick that we needed to really work on getting the house ready to show. He said, "The house looks great!" I said, "It looks great if someone lives here, but we have to act like no one lives here!" It's just like an Instagram post showing the perfect life, the perfect picture. Delete all the ones with your eyes closed and your kids picking their nose. Those moments didn't happen; let's forget about those. That was basically how I grew up. I remember every adult that I ever ran into as a child mentioning our family's Christmas card. Someone would see us in the Grove at an Ole Miss game and say, "Joan, you have the three most gorgeous girls! Your Christmas cards!" Well, yes, we always had a fabulous Christmas card. I cannot imagine how many hours my sweet mom spent hand-smocking our three dresses, stitching the lace, and hemming it herself so they looked pristine. My mom did it all. She cooked all day, was an interior designer, and made our house a home. Even though my parents were not happily married, and we could feel that, she did everything she possibly could to make our life feel perfect for us. I resented this for some reason as a child, and now, I completely get it. I find myself yelling at my kids, "*Put on the belt for the Christmas card!*" We all do it!

My sweet friend Liz Banfield is an incredibly talented photographer. Whenever she comes in town, she asks to shoot my kids' portraits. Well, there is never a perfect time for the Christmas card, right? Their hair isn't right, because Grace used Sun In and it is orange, and Walker's loafers are too small. I do not have the perfect outfits ready to put the perfect image of our life into the world. Why do we do this? Why does this make us feel better? But it does. I think it has something to do with how if everything appears to be OK, even if the kitchen is on fire, you can get through it. If you show the mess that is going on inside you, it's all over.

- Do you feel this way? Have you ever put up walls because if you face what's behind them, you will crumble? Let it out right here:

    _____

    _____

    _____

    _____

I laugh when I say "kitchen on fire," because I have had this happen at a wedding. During my entire planning career, people said, "You are so calm." Little did they know that the kitchen was actually on fire. I learned from the best: my mom. She did it all in the most gracious Southern way, even when the kitchen was on fire.

If the Kitchen Is On Fire, Keep Smiling!

Here's a little background on the bride and groom's wedding that actually caught on fire. We will call the bride "Glenda." Glenda was type A, to say the least. We spoke several times a day, and I even spoke to her fiancé a few more times a day than I spoke to her. They needed a full-time wedding planner, assistant, best friend, and 24/7 confidant. By most people's standards, they were crazy. But I genuinely liked them. This is another reason you yourself must be a little crazy if you want to be an event planner! They had over-the-top ideas, and I found it exciting and energizing to try and bring these ideas to life and make the bride and groom happy. I spent late nights at the office analyzing every detail to make sure it was perfect. I remember one winter night, I was about to leave the office, and the landline phone rang. "Hey there, got a sec?" I heard on the other line. It was Daniel, the groom. I glanced out the window, and it was so dark that I could not see the cars in the parking lot. I thought to myself, *It's right now or tomorrow, so sit down and buckle up!*

He always needed to talk through every single detail that was going through his mind. For any possible situation that could occur or cause worry about the wedding, he would call me. Today, he was having trouble writing his wedding speech to his fiancée for his toast and needed some help. After an hour of being on the phone with him listening to his toast, rewriting his toast, and adding in jokes, he finally said we could talk again tomorrow. The funny thing about being a wedding planner is the client feels like you are the only one they can talk to about things. Many times, they do not want their friends to know the details of the wedding because they want them to be surprised when they come to the wedding, and they do not want anyone to get wind of the details ahead of time and steal the ideas. That would be terrible! So, the details are pretty hush-hush—not to mention to make sure their friends don't realize how crazy they really are or how crazy their mother really is. Better to just talk to the wedding planner; surely, she has seen it all and is paid to tell you that you are not crazy, right?! Ha. I was paid to be a best friend and counselor. I always joked that my business card should just read "therapist." Weddings and funerals—you are dealing with people at the most emotional time of their lives.

The wedding weekend was here, and the bride was so incredibly worried about every single detail. Were her friends going to wear the perfect outfit? Was her new mother-in-law going to say the right thing? Was the food going to be the exact recipes we gave the caterer? Were the flowers going to be white and not ivory? Were the butterflies going to fly out of the boxes at exactly the right time and not die? So many worries and so much anxiety, and I was the one telling them the entire time it was all going to be OK! But was it? I made some big promises, and now I had to deliver! Of course, I was worried about how we were going to all get through this, but I could not show my inner worry. I had to smile, lead, and keep going!

The day of the wedding, the ceremony was perfect! The ceremony had so many intricate details, and if we could get through that, surely the rest of the night would go smoothly as well. That is one lesson I have learned the hard way. *Do not*—I repeat, *do not*—pat yourself on the back until *everything* is over, until every guest has left, and maybe even wait until the next day. You cannot let your guard down, because that is when things happen—or at least, that's my experience.

All the guests had arrived at the reception, and the cars were being parked by the valet team. The location was a beautiful antebellum building with floor-to-ceiling columns separating the mezzanine and gorgeous crystal chandeliers running down the center of the ceiling. The twenty-four-piece string orchestra was playing as guests entered the room, and our team greeted the guests with gold-leafed name cards that we cut off giant trees for the guests to keep as a takeaway favor. The guests were greeted with Cristal champagne in gold-rimmed flutes as every detail was falling into place. It should be, as we had talked through every detail endlessly and planned for every possible thing that could go wrong! Except for this …

The band was Earth, Wind & Fire. Right as they were playing their iconic song that made them so popular, "September," I heard the fire alarm sound. The red lights on the walls of the building were

the THROUGH *line*

flashing red, and the loud *beep, beep, beep* was piercing. I thought to myself, *You have got to be kidding me! Of course, of all weddings, of all brides, this wedding* cannot *be on fire!* I decided to quickly get to the bottom of this before we had everyone evacuate. If it was a false alarm, maybe the party could keep going! I was not going to let this party stop unless I had to! I was next to the dance floor and spotted the bride and groom centered on the dance floor right next to the stage, dancing. From the dance floor, the music was so loud, and the flashing red lights actually blended in with the light show of the band. I waved at the sound guy and yelled, "*Turn it up!*" I pierced my eyes at the lighting technician and said, "Keep flashing the lights like in the biggest light show, like a finale! I don't want anyone to see the alarms going off." I had to act fast, because if there was a fire and we did need to evacuate and get these guests out of there, then of course, safety first! But it was my job to analyze the danger of the situation without disturbing the party. Go! Run!

I ran into the kitchen, and the manager said, "I have good news and bad news. The good news is there is not a real fire. The bad news is the fire department has to come with a key to get into this closet to turn off the fire alarm, and we have to wait until they get here, and we cannot do anything." "Are you kidding me!" I grumbled. "Of all weddings, you have to turn this off. If a fire doesn't kill me today, this bride *definitely* will kill me if fire alarms and flashing lights ruined her wedding." And I was not ready to die that day! "Ma'am, there is nothing we can do." I ran as fast as I could back to the dance floor. The guests that were not by the dance floor were looking around, wondering what was happening. I smiled my *biggest* cheerleader smile. I saw their eyebrows drop, and the guests seemed not to worry as if I could read their minds. "If the wedding planner in that black dress with the walkie-talkie isn't worried about the fire alarm, then I am going to grab another vodka tonic and not worry either!" It worked every time. If I was calm, then the room was calm. I raced to the bar and grabbed a scotch on the rocks for the groom and a champagne for the bride.

I ran to the dance floor, and as I approached, I saw the groom leaving. I said, "Hi, where are you going?" He said, "To take my coat off!" I said, "Give me your coat! I will take it for you, and here is another drink. You just go back out on the dance floor and enjoy tonight, and I will do all the work!" His eyes gleamed at me as if to say thank you, and he turned around. *Whew.* That was a close one. How did they not hear the alarm and think it was part of the band? In any case, I was going to stand there and make sure they did not leave the dance floor. Out of the corner of my eye, I saw movement on the mezzanine. I glanced up and saw five firemen in their heavy fire coats walking down the mezzanine briskly, holding axes. *Axes!* Really?! You couldn't have left those in the fire truck? Good Lord. The firemen approached the closet and actually used the ax to break into the door and then turned the key off. Thank you, thank you! If we could get through the fire alarm without the bride and groom knowing, surely we could get through anything this night threw at me!

Chapter One Takeaways and Reflections

I believe we can all learn from stories like these, even in the craziest of times. Whether it was when my daughter was very sick or when I thought the wedding was on fire, I tried to remain calm. I tried to take a minute to pause and assess the situation. I made a diagram in my head.

What is the path I can take to get the best result here? If I am calm and authentic with the people in front of me, how can I get to where I want to be by leading with my heart and not getting too worked up?

Quarterbacks are doing this constantly. They have a play called, but what if that person isn't open? What if there are other people in the way blocking that play from happening?

This is life, and we are the quarterbacks of our own life. We think we may have a playbook, and I may have had a detailed wedding timeline, but the moment comes when it's time to throw the ball. We have to make quick decisions based on all of our experience, to take all of that experience and wisdom and sometimes make split-second decisions that will affect the rest of our life. How prepared do you feel to make these decisions?

Do you trust yourself? Do you have someone to bounce these ideas off of? For me, it is my husband, my mom, and my sister. I like to run every decision by them. I truly do think that when more minds work together, the views and opinions will also be the best. We were not born just knowing what to do in every situation. We must constantly be learning from others and having others keep us in check if necessary.

It all goes back to being *Present Over Perfect*, one of my favorite books by Shauna Niequist. It is funny that I met her early on in my event-planning career. She was an amazing event planner herself who changed her own life completely. She saw this need for change much earlier than I did. I loved her book and everything she said, it just took me longer to get there.

Questions to Ask Yourself

- Can you think of situations you have been in where you had to think fast, make big decisions, and assess which route to take? What did you learn about yourself in those moments?

  _____
  _____
  _____

- How can you be more authentic in your life?

  _____
  _____
  _____

- How can you be more present in your life and stop worrying about being perfect?

  _____
  _____
  _____

I am trying every day in my life to follow this motto: one day at a time, be authentic, be yourself, don't worry about others, and happiness will follow.

Chapter Two

SHIFTING GEARS TO OVERCOME CHALLENGES

Adaptability and the Transformative Power of Resilience in the Face of Challenges

> *The greatest discovery of all time is that a person can change his future by merely changing his attitude.*
>
> —OPRAH WINFREY

Fast forward to November 15, 2021. I was in a meeting, and my phone was on silent. I try to put my phone away during meetings to be present with each client. When we finished the meeting, I reached for my purse and grabbed my phone. I had fifteen missed calls from my kids' elementary school and from Merrick. My stomach completely sank to the floor. I immediately called Merrick, and he said, "You need to come right away. Something is terribly wrong with Grace; just get to school as fast as you can." Why did I not have my phone out? How did I miss all these calls? Merrick had arrived at the school first and went into the room with Grace, but she did not know who he was. I approached the front door of the school, and they did not even make me sign in. There was a row of teachers and staff down the hall, looking at me as if someone had died and just pointing to the room at the end of the hallway. As I approached the room, I saw that the lights were off, and the room was dark. Grace was crawling around on the floor acting like a toddler or an animal. She did not know who Merrick was, but she did recognize me. Her teachers that she had known for a few years, she did not recognize. Suddenly, she looked outside the window and saw a giant oak tree and started screaming in the most terrifying, loud shrieks you could imagine. She genuinely thought the tree was going to come through the window and attack her.

Something was terribly wrong, but we did not know what it was. I was able to get her into my car in the front seat. I pushed the gear shift into reverse to back out of the parking lot. As I drove forward for thirty seconds, she pushed the stick shift as hard as she could into reverse and then into park. My car jolted forward on the busy two-lane road, and I was scared to drive. I could not do this alone. I knew I needed to drive to the hospital, but there was no way I could make it there on the toll road with her pushing the gears into park. I drove three blocks to our house and pulled into the alleyway to the garage. As I opened the garage, Grace said, "Where are we?" with a genuinely terrified shrill. "Where are you taking me? Please do not kidnap me! Please take me to my parents." At this moment, I realized she did not know who I was. Merrick opened the back door as I pulled the car into the garage, and our two-year-old fox red lab ran out the door. You would have thought her favorite dog was a lion. She screamed and screamed and ran out of the car and actually started to climb up the walls as if to run away from the dog like a cat would climb a tree. I could see how truly scared she was, so scared that she would not go inside our house.

Chapter Two: Shifting Gears to Overcome Challenges

Little did I know that our family's entire life was about to change. When you are in that moment and your own ten-year-old daughter is so terrified and desperate, you are also terrified. My daughter just the day before was in a cheer competition and did ten back handsprings all while smiling, dancing, and living her best life with her team.

We drove to the emergency room. Doctor after doctor came into her room and just looked at her and told us they had never seen anything like this, and maybe we should see a psychiatrist. A psychiatrist? That is for anxiety medicine! My daughter had no clue who I was, and yesterday she was perfectly normal! We needed more than a psychiatrist; we needed a neurologist. We were sent home with a phone number of a psychiatrist and their parting look of "Good luck!" We were frightened and felt hopeless.

The wedding planner in me was the perfect training for being told no at the hospital. You can't tell me no … do you know who you are dealing with? No is not an acceptable answer. It is 2023, and we live in Dallas, Texas, with some of the best healthcare in the country. There was a solution; I just needed to find the person that had it. I called every neurologist that I could find. Most had a waiting list of six months or required a recommendation from another doctor, and since the ER had released us, I did not have that. Grace was home from school and would have seizures out of nowhere.

I could not leave her alone, much less make a phone call longer than two minutes, so finding a doctor was not an easy feat. Suddenly, Grace's eyes would roll in the back of her head, and she would fall to the floor, then she would stand up, open the back door, run into the backyard, and try to jump in the pool while in an episode. I could not handle this. I called Dr. Majeed, who was recommended to me from a friend. I had called him several times before and had an appointment for January. I could not wait two months, as we did not have two months. His nurse answered with a beautiful Polish accent. I was crying—not hysterically, just genuinely at-the-bottom-of-my-hopeless-rope tears. I had nowhere else to go. I could not go back to the ER, and no other neurologists were accepting children. I begged and begged her and told her I had nowhere else to turn. She put me on hold as I watched Grace pass out on the sofa. This would often happen after an episode, where she would pass out. The woman came back to the phone and said, "Well, I do not believe it myself. In seven years, I have never seen Dr. Majeed do this, but he said if you can come right now, he will see you." It was 4:00 p.m. I picked up Grace and escorted her to the car. Merrick had left to pick up Walker from school.

I headed down our street and saw them walking toward me. I rolled down the window and said, "Hop in! We must go right this minute." We drove to the doctor's office. Grace was comatose. We went into the patient room, and she laid down on the table, completely passed out. Dr. Majeed walked in and sat down calmly and looked at Merrick and me. He could see how frightened we were. He could see how helpless we were. He looked in our eyes and we knew he was really listening. We knew he cared. He said, "Tell me everything." We explained to him what had been happening, and after about thirty minutes, he said, "I believe your daughter has what is called autoimmune encephalitis."

We looked at each other and then looked at him in confusion. I asked for a pen and the spelling of what he had just diagnosed. I had never heard of such a thing. We told him how the other doctors had never seen this before. He looked at us with such warmth in his eyes, but also a deep sorrow at the same time. He knew the road we had ahead of us. He said, "I have just seen a zebra before, that is all. If you had never seen a zebra before, and people told you there was a horse with black stripes, you probably would not believe it. I have seen this, and this is serious. You need to immediately go check into the ICU. I will call the emergency room and have them send you directly to the ICU on the top floor." I knew something was very wrong, but the ICU?! I looked at him and said, "Now? Can we go home and pack a bag?" He looked at us in shock and said, "I do not know why you would wait; you need to go now!" We drove across the interstate to the hospital. They knew we were coming, and some team members met us outside the electric doors with a bed. They immediately whisked her onto the bed, started an IV, and did a spinal tap. How did this all happen so quickly? Finally, finally, someone was listening.

For the past two years, I had been working on an incredibly detailed wedding in Jamaica. It was one of those weddings that was not like anything else. The bride was a designer and was very detailed. The family had roots in Jamaica for generations, and it was such a special place to them. We had been working on the wedding for so long because we had planned the wedding and then COVID happened. We had already moved the wedding date three times. After four trips to Jamaica, with custom block-printed linens, every detail perfectly curated, and midnight Zoom calls with vendors in four different countries, nothing was going to stop us from making this wedding perfect. I would have done anything to make that wedding perfect. I had spent countless hours on Zoom calls during the pandemic in the closet preparing this wedding while simultaneously homeschooling my kids. This wedding had every single detail thought through, and it was going to be perfect. I would not have missed it for the world.

The night we ended up in the ICU was a Monday night. I was supposed to be on a 7:00 a.m. flight the next morning to Jamaica for the actual wedding week. The first event was not until Thursday. I texted the mother of the bride and said, "I wanted to let you know that my daughter is in the hospital, and I will not be on the flight in the morning. But do not worry, because I will be there by the Thursday night party." I completely believed that. I also had no idea what the next few days, weeks, months, and years held.

> **PRO TIP**
>
> *Learn to think and stay present in the minutes, hours, and days and not get overwhelmed with the future and what we cannot control.*

Life is funny that way. If you knew what the next days, weeks, and months held, you just might not be able to get through it. If I have learned anything, I have learned to live one day at a time. That's truly the biggest life lesson after all of this. I am a planner. I plan my life out years in advance. I could tell you what I am doing in a year on a Saturday in November, because my life has been planned out that far in advance for twenty years.

It took a life-altering situation with my daughter to wake me up, to see what is really important, to embrace authenticity, to appreciate people, to love my people.

It is crazy how God puts people in your life at the right time. This client was extremely detailed. We had hundreds of conversations about the color green. Seriously. We talked and talked about lines on palm leaves and how they are shaded green. And I listened, gave my opinion, and wanted them to be so happy with the perfect palm leaf shading. So having to call them to tell them my daughter was in the hospital was also terrifying.

The second I called, Leslie, the mother of the bride said, "Do not come; do not get on that plane." I could not believe what I was hearing. But I had to be there; I would do anything to be there. Leslie had lost a child. Her son had passed away in a hazing accident in college. She knew the helpless feeling that was running through my veins. She knew that she would give anything to hug her son one more time. She said she would not let me get on the plane. Wow. To put her in my life at that moment when I was so afraid to upset them and only wanted the wedding to be perfect … but I also knew that I could not leave Grace and my family. This put my mind at ease. My team went to Jamaica and flawlessly executed the wedding. All the countless hours of planning on the front end paid off, and the execution was perfect. I was so relieved.

I never left the hospital. After the first few days, only one test came back positive. It was for COVID antibodies. What did that mean? The doctors explained that most likely, Grace had COVID before, and the antibodies went to her brain, and her immune system began attacking her own brain cells. What? How is that possible? We never knew she had COVID, and she never had any symptoms. Well, evidently, you can also get encephalitis from strep throat. It is very rare, one in a million. Why could we not have won the lottery, which is also a very rare event, instead? I wanted her to be better. I wanted to grasp at anything to fix her. The doctors had a plan. They would give her steroids and IVIG. They called it "liquid gold." They said she was lucky to get that, because it would give her the best of the best antibodies, and she would never get sick again! I felt relieved to have a diagnosis and a plan.

We had been so self-consumed the past few days and honestly had just been getting through the days. It was like when you have your first baby and look up at the clock and it's 4:00 p.m., and you realized you haven't brushed your teeth yet and you are still in your PJs, and it is almost time to put them back on. Do you remember those days? You just get through them.

The God Moments

In the children's ICU, we shared a nurse and wall with a next-door neighbor. I had peeked in the room next door and saw a sweet young girl who looked about seven years of age. I could only see the right side of her face and could tell she was on some type of breathing machine. Her mom never left her side and laid with her like a blanket draped over her, just staring at her for days, crying. We knew something serious was going on but did not have the chance to speak and did not want to intrude. One night, Grace had a very hard night. Because of her condition, we had a technician in the room twenty-four hours a day for support. Every day was a different person, and it was a lot to have someone in the small room with you at all times. That night at the 7:00 p.m. shift change, our night tech walked in the door. Her name was Rhonda, and she was full of life. When she walked in, she commanded the room, almost like she was giving a sermon that we all felt like we needed after a long day. She started talking to Grace about God and how when she is scared and has no idea what to do, she needs to just talk to God. She talked to Grace about how to do that and told her that He will listen.

In that moment of sweet Rhonda and Grace's hours of conversation and bonding, I thought to myself, maybe this is why we are here: to bring us closer to God and closer together as a family. That night, Rhonda gave Grace a nice coin that she had always carried with her everywhere. It is called the "Armor of God." She told Grace to carry it with her wherever she goes, and it will remind her that God is with her, and she can talk to him. That night, the coin and Rhonda calmed Grace's worries, and she held tight to the coin and slept.

The next day, we saw a team of fifteen doctors go in the room next door. We didn't know what was happening to the little girl, but it made our heart hurt. Grace was having a better day and said, "Mom, I think the girl in the room next to us, Ebby, needs this coin more than I do." She wrote a note and passed it to the nurses outside the door and asked them to give the coin and letter to Ebby to hold.

The next day, I passed the parents in the lobby. We had never spoken before, but I recognized her. The mom was crying much harder than before, and I could tell I should not interrupt them, but something was telling me to go over to her. I did. I just said, "Can I hug you?" She said yes, and we hugged for what seemed like a long while. I sat down, and she told me her seven-year-old daughter was being put on a ventilator at that moment. My heart sank to the floor. I had just gone through my father being put on a ventilator in September, which he never woke up from, and I knew the severity of the situation. While I had just gone through this, it was my father. He had lived a wonderful sixty-five years. This was her sweet seven-year-old innocent baby. I didn't leave. I couldn't leave. I felt that we were both there in that place together for a reason.

Over the next few days and weeks, our friendship grew. It was one of the first times a stranger had been put in my life where I clearly knew we were both in that same exact place and that same exact moment for a reason. She needed me, and I needed her. The interesting thing about being in a crisis is your friends and family mean so well and try to help, and they do. But there is something comforting about being with or talking to someone who has walked in your shoes.

As Grace became better, we found out we could go home the next day. I was hoping Rhonda would be our night shift tech. I went to the administration desk and asked, "Could I please request Rhonda to be our technician tonight? It is our last night here, and she was so wonderful to our family."

"Ma'am," the woman behind the desk said with a confused look. "There is no one by the name of Rhonda that works here in the ICU, and definitely not a night tech." I was mystified, and to this day, I believe Rhonda was our angel that gave us what God knew we needed in that moment.

Grace was released from the hospital, and Ebby stayed. She was on a ventilator for twelve long days. I felt a little guilty going home. It was like all the gifts and flowers didn't matter, knowing that Ebby's family and so many others were still in the hospital.

Counting Our Blessings and Adapting to the New Normal

We felt so thankful to be home for Thanksgiving Day. It gave an entirely new perspective to going around the table and saying what you are thankful for. And the doctors were not kidding about the liquid gold! Grace seemed like the best version of herself. She seemed perfectly normal for ten days. We had gone to the lake for Thanksgiving for some quiet family time, about an hour southeast of Dallas. It was nice to be out in nature with the sounds of the birds instead of the constant sound of beeping from the machines. I do not know how doctors and nurses get used to the constant beeping. It raises your heart rate just hearing that.

It was getting later in the day the Saturday of Thanksgiving. We had a full day of turkey, rice, green bean casserole, and football games. My heart was so full. I was doing the dishes in the kitchen as I looked over and saw Grace on the floor. I ran over to her, and her eyes were glazed over, and her pupils were rolled back in her head, and she asked me who I was. How could this be? We had had the best few days together. The nightmare was over, wasn't it? This could not be happening. We tried to get her to stand up, and her legs were like jelly, and she fell to the ground. I sat with her as she begged me to take her to her parents. I did not want her to be scared, so I assured her we would find them and she would be safe. She said she knew exactly where I could find her father's number; it was on a billboard on Lovers Lane and the tollway.

My heart sank. She described a family that I was an acquaintance of, and his number was on that billboard. But we did not really know them. How could she think this was her family when I had done everything in the world for her? How could she not know me? I could not make this moment about my feelings and instead had to make her feel safe. We FaceTimed her neurologist, and he advised us to give her rescue medicine to help her to go to sleep, and hopefully, when she woke up in the morning, she would be OK. We would use what we called rescue medicine as a last resort in desperate times, which essentially just knocked her out. It was heartbreaking to give this to your own child.

She finally fell asleep. We were so frightened. We were an hour away from the hospital, and it was late and dark outside. The best thing to do was to go to sleep and see how she was in the morning. Surely this was just a setback and not a relapse.

Merrick and I laid in bed with one eye opened all night. We could not sleep with the fear of what was happening. At 4:55 a.m., we heard a loud thump. We sprang up and ran into Grace's room. She was on the floor. She had tried to stand up out of bed, and her legs just did not work. She looked at me in the eyes and tried to speak. Her mouth moved and she mouthed words, but no sound came out. My eyes welled up with tears. I scooped her up, carrying her like a baby, and ran to the car. I did not even grab my shoes, I just ran. I sat in the back seat with her on the hour-long car ride.

Merrick drove about 95 mph on the interstate, and I thought to myself, *She is either dying from what is happening to her or we won't even make it to the hospital because we are all going to die in a car accident.* I had never been so scared in my life. We were running on fumes. This was out of our control. I called our neurologist that we had become so attached to. We trusted him, and he had led us in the right direction the past few weeks. I was trying to balance holding Grace up in her seat while answering hospital calls at the same time to get us into the hospital. Dr. Majeed called me back, and I could tell from the tone of his voice it was not good news.

He said, "There are not any beds at Medical City Children's; you need to go to another hospital." I said, "But can you be our doctor at another hospital? Because we only want you." He said, "Unfortunately, no. But there are other great doctors out there." I cried, "But you are the one that has seen the zebra. We need you! Let me make a call, and I will call you right back." Here comes the planner in me. Do not tell me no. I can fix this. I called a mother from my son's elementary school that also happened to be the president of the Children's Hospital. I did not know her well, but she had come to see us in the hospital, and it was a small community. I told her the situation and that we were driving to the hospital now. We needed Dr. Majeed and our nurses; we needed Rhonda. Please help us! She said in a sympathetic voice, "Sara Fay, there just are not any beds available; you have to go to another hospital." I thought to myself, *We live in one of the best cities in one of the best countries in the world with the best healthcare, and there is not a bed available in the children's hospital. This is a problem.*

But This Can't Happen to Me

This is something you think will never happen to you. Truly, think about it. Don't you think if you are sick, you could get to a doctor?

That you could be admitted and find a hospital bed? Never in a million years had it crossed my mind there would not be enough beds or staff to treat us. Once again, everything happened for a reason.

We drove to Children's Health in Dallas and drove straight to the emergency room. It felt like we were starting over. "Name, date of birth," the lady at the check-in desk was saying. I said, "We need a wheelchair." I grabbed the nearest wheelchair by the sliding doors and rolled it out to the car as Merrick picked up Grace, still without shoes on, and put her in the wheelchair. She had been walking toward me so fast, and her mouth was moving so fast, but still, nothing was coming out. I raced the wheelchair as fast as I could into the waiting room. Merrick had to drive the dog home and get us shoes since we had left in a panic, so I felt all alone in that moment. This time, the staff in the ER realized the severity of our situation and rolled us back into another room. While trying to get all our records and tests transferred to this hospital, all the tests started over again. "Ma'am, we need to do our own testing." I understood, but this sweet child didn't need another lumbar puncture. She shouldn't even know what a lumbar puncture is. She shouldn't know when they come in to draw her blood that she needs to request the IV team, because they get the vein on the first try.

I glanced at the door and pictured her friends right this minute at cheer practice, tumbling, feeling free without a care in the world, and my heart hurt. Why her; why us? There must be a reason behind this, a purpose for all this. Have you ever felt that way? Like, why is this happening to you? Grace interrupted my daydreaming by telling the IV team, "I want a J-Tip." She had learned that a J-Tip is the miracle spray that the nurses can spray on your skin so you do not feel an IV or blood draw. We learned *all* the tricks. One day, Grace can write the book on hospital survival for kids, highlighting the French fries, service dogs, Ryan Seacrest studio, and J-Tips!

After a few days and what seemed like an eternity, we had a plan for the second phase of encephalitis treatment. It was called plasmapheresis. What? What in the world is that? The doctor said, "Picture a washing machine. It is a washing machine for the blood. We will put a port in her neck. It will pull her blood out and through the machine and will sort the bad plasma from the good plasma. The good plasma and good blood will go right back into her body as soon as it comes out, and the bad plasma will be discarded. Just like washing your clothes; it is like washing your blood!" She had said it so matter-of-factly, like we were doing laundry. This all seemed so surreal. But we had a plan. As long as we had someone with a higher education in this medical treatment and this person had also "seen a zebra," I knew I had to trust them.

The surgery to put the port in her neck was scary. Seeing the port in her neck was sad. I was just sad for her. But I did not have time to be sad. I needed to be her cheerleader. I needed to bring joy into this hospital room. I had never witnessed the true love and generosity of friends as I did in this moment and time in the hospital. People that I barely knew, friends of friends, acquaintances, neighbors, an extended network beyond what we knew, and also our close friends and family—they all rallied around us. That parable called "Footprints" of the little girl walking on the beach who says: "God, where were you during this difficult time? I only see one set of footprints, and not two," and He says, "Because I was carrying you"—this is how I felt. Our entire family was completely carried through this time. I had never felt the importance of friends and family as in that moment. Our friends even built a chimney for Grace's hospital room so Santa could come and made a Christmas tree for her room with handmade cards as ornaments from all of Grace's friends—the sweetest handmade notes you have ever seen!

This is what it is all about. Had I been too busy to be this kind of friend to others? Would I have reached out to a stranger if they were in this position or just thought, "Oh, I do not know them that well; it would be weird if I reach out." Have you ever found yourself wondering that? I learned after this to always reach out. It does not matter if you are a complete stranger. Write the letter, send the flowers, show up. The people that show up will be remembered and make a difference; I promise.

Ebby and her mom would check on us every day. Christmas was approaching. The tables had completely turned as we thought Ebby would be in the hospital for Christmas, and instead, here we were. They offered to bring us Christmas dinner and gifts. We didn't want them to do anything but spend time together, since they thought they would be the ones in the hospital. On Christmas Eve, we got special permission for Walker, Merrick, and I to have dinner in the hospital cafeteria with Grace, even though only one guest was allowed due to the COVID rules. My mother and sister decorated our table and brought us food from our favorite restaurant. Sitting there on Christmas Eve, I could have been in a thousand other places at that moment, but my heart was so full right there with my family in the hospital cafeteria.

Grace wasn't feeling well, so we wheeled her back up to the room after a short dinner. When we turned into the room, there was an envelope on her bed. It was from Ebby. Tears welled in my eyes. Grace quickly tore open the envelope, and out fell the coin that Grace had given to her at the other hospital. Her letter said, "Grace, I am all better now and am praying for you. You now need this coin more than I do. Hold on to it tight, and I am excited to meet you one day when you are home and all better. Merry Christmas. Love, Ebby."

Ebby and Grace had never met, but this authentic bond between these two girls was real. It was teaching them something about humanity, about goodness, about love.

Shifting Gears when You Cannot Control the People around You

It is almost laughable to think about how many times I have had to shift gears to overcome challenges—I would say in event planning, almost with every event. But looking back, this skill set helped me with so many things that life threw my way, and instead of getting too upset or knocked down, I just found another way and kept going. I think also not overthinking or worrying is the best plan. When you worry too much about things out of your control, all you are doing is causing anxiety and fear about something you can do nothing about.

I have so many wedding stories that would relate to switching gears. One of my favorites included President George W. Bush while he was the sitting president. While working for Todd Events, I was planning a very special wedding for the sweetest bride at her home in Maine. The Bushes were very close friends of hers, and Jenna and Barbara Bush were bridesmaids. The Bushes are some of the most thoughtful people and did not want the wedding to be about them. They wanted it to be about the bride. The president knew that if he planned to attend the wedding, there would have to be metal detectors, background checks, and many levels of security that the bride probably did not dream about for her wedding day. The week went on as we set up the bridge over the pool to serve as the aisle for the bride to walk across. During the entire setup that week, we had

Secret Service present to watch the building, since the First Lady and the First Daughters would be in attendance.

One of my favorite parts about weddings is, again, you guessed it, the people. You really get to know the people. I adored this bride. The first time I met her, it was like a slumber party. We stayed up talking and looking at *Us* magazine like we were in a sorority house. When you spend trips with days and nights together over a period of a year, usually you become close with the families. Getting to know people so well helps to take those special elements of their lives and infuse them into the details of the wedding to make it uniquely theirs. So, for this wedding, I knew the family, the specific players, and where their assigned seats were for the ceremony. The wedding day had finally arrived with the most beautiful crisp August Maine weather. Everything was going perfectly. The strings were playing in the backyard as guests were arriving at the bride's parents' home. About half of the seats were full when the bride's brother walked up to me and whispered in my ear, "Do not freak out, but the president is on his way." He continued, "He will walk in just before the grandparents as part of the processional and will sit on the aisle with the family next to the First Lady. The seat next to her that we told you was for the Secret Service is really for the president."

I smiled, although I was totally panicking on the inside and running through the list of all things to do in this moment through my head. But on the outside, I had to show professionalism and grace. All eyes were on me as the guests looked back at the house. The next few minutes went very quickly as President Bush arrived, and I shook his hand and turned toward the steps down to the pool and said, "Right this way, Mr. President." As he continued to follow me, I turned and glanced down the aisle to where the two seats were reserved. Out of the corner of my eye, I saw that there was a bright red dress sitting in the seat that was reserved for the president. I briskly whipped around to President Bush and said, "Just one moment, Mr. President!" As the strings played, all eyes were on me as they were expecting the family processional and now President Bush was in full sight of all the guests. I carefully walked down the stairs to the pool so as not to fall, smiling the entire time. I guess it is the Southern girl in me, but I am such a people pleaser that I always know if I smile and the guests begin to smile back, I can win them over, even in crisis.

I approached the woman in the candy-apple-red dress and said, "Excuse me, but this seat is reserved. If you could kindly move over to the other reserved seats right over there, that would be great!" She looked at me in all seriousness and said, "But I am family." Again, I knew the key players, and I did not know who this woman was. I said with a smile, "Well, there is a family row right over there, so please move." She would not budge and crossed her arms as she grunted, "Well, who is this seat reserved for?" With my best smile and broadcaster voice I replied, "Mr. and Mrs. Bush." And the woman quickly said, "*Well*, they are *not* family." I could not believe my ears. All eyes are on me, and this woman will not move. By this point, I have figured out this must be the aunt that invited herself a few weeks before that no one wanted to come. It is always the aunt in the red dress—ha!

Think fast, Sara Fay. This woman cannot tell you no. There is always a solution. This is for the sitting president of the United States of America, and everyone is watching! So, I took a deep breath and smiled even bigger as to let the words come through my teeth without even moving my lips and said, "There are snipers in those trees right over there with guns pointed at this exact seat, and if you do not move, I will radio the snipers. Now please move, and thank you!" She stood up and knocked over a few people with her purse as she eloquently waddled to her new seat. I then smiled a sincere and satisfactory smile as I turned to the president and Mrs. Bush and waved them to come to their seats. There is always a way. And a smile is usually in the recipe to get you there—a smile, gumption, and not taking no for an answer. I always giggle a little when people yell and then do not get their way. Have you ever seen a grown man yell, not get his way, and then continue to act like a toddler? Instead, a smile usually does the trick.

Customs Nightmare

Another one of my favorite "shifting gears" stories was actually from our dear friends Eli Manning and Abby McGrew's wedding. They were close family friends, which always adds a little more pressure, because while I want things to be perfect for every client, when it is friends, you want it to be even more special. It was April 2007, and Eli had just led the Giants in a Super Bowl win against the Patriots the February before. There were even more eyes and attention on him after this huge feat. The Wednesday before the wedding, I stood in the ballroom in Mexico, where we were preparing all the flowers. Usually, we receive the flowers for a wedding on the Wednesday before the wedding and would process the flowers by cleaning them, clipping them, and putting the stems in water to let them open to be in the most perfect condition by Saturday. It was getting later in the day on Wednesday, and the flowers still had not arrived.

It is much harder to import flowers into Mexico because the country has very strict rules at customs regarding which flowers can and cannot be accepted into the country. This makes it tricky for planning the flower arrangements for weddings since you are limited in your choices. A wedding in the United States on the same date as a wedding in Mexico may not be able to have the same flowers, even if they are in season, because of these strict rules. Good thing we had an incredible team and only ordered flowers off the approved list. I was feeling great about the week until the phone rang that moment as I was staring at the clock. It was our lead floral designer, who just received the call that the customs agent had burned the flowers when they were crossing the border. What? How is that possible? Well, they do not have to give you an answer. They could have seen a bug, so they burned them. Or who knows, maybe one of the customs agents had a daughter getting married and decided they needed them more than us. We will never know. But we had to act fast. We were in Cabo, so there was not a floral market close by. There was no other option. But I was not about to go tell my friends that they did not have flowers for their wedding. We had to redirect. The bride loved orchids and wanted orchids hanging from the ceiling. At this point, we would be lucky to have anything besides a cactus, much less orchids.

We decided to send two of our floral designers on a flight to Mexico City to go to the flower market. We had them grab all the flowers they could, rent a U-Haul, and drive down to Cabo with the flowers they had gathered. It was down to the wire. I had to smile to the guests, my friends, and family and pretend like all was OK. I knew it would be, and there was no sense in worrying anyone. It was my job to worry. It was my job to redirect and find a solution. That is what your clients are paying you for anyway, so they can be guests at their own wedding and not stress. The wedding ended up being absolutely stunning. Our amazing teams worked overnight to get everything done. Most everything ended up being exactly what they wanted. The only different element was that instead of orchids hanging from the ceiling, it was roses. But it was gorgeous, and no one ever knew the drama that took place behind the scenes. I finally told Abby and Eli a few years ago, and now we can look back and laugh.

What is the process for staying calm in the moment? Some key tools that have helped me include stopping to breathe. Take a minute to collect your thoughts. How can you take a brief moment in your mind to process the situation before giving a solution or reacting? My mind scans all options, and I start throwing out options. If time allows, I always run things by my trusted advisors, team, or Merrick. I feel like when I can talk through my why and say it out loud, it helps me to realize if it is the right or wrong step to take. It is funny when you say something to a trusted advisor; sometimes they do not have to give a reply. You just know by saying it out loud what the right thing to do is and what they would say in response to you. That is my system for pulling it together and identifying specific steps to take to go forward. Breathe, pull together your thoughts, listen to your inner voice (even if someone is speaking loudly about what they think you should do), shift your focus to the situation, and put it all together.

Events to Restaurant Management Overnight

One of my biggest shifting of gears involved changing my career-long journey of events and wedding planning to managing restaurants. This shift happened overnight, was unplanned, and was emotional, to say the least.

I had just left the musical *Wicked* with girlfriends. I looked at my phone and had several missed calls from a number that I did not recognize. The same number had called me the night before, but I was setting up an event and had not had a chance to listen to the voicemail. I got in the back seat of my friend's car and buckled up as my phone rang again. It was the same 713 number, so I answered, "Hello?" and a somewhat familiar voice came through the other line. "Sara Fay, this is Oscar. I have been trying to get in touch with you."

Oscar was my dad's director of culinary operations for the restaurants for many years and his closest friend. He traveled with him everywhere. He deeply cared for my dad like a father figure. "Your father begged me not to call you, but he is very sick, and he is in the hospital with COVID, and you need to know."

"What?" I exclaimed. "But he was better! I knew he was sick a week ago, but I thought he was at home now and doing OK." The last conversation I had with my dad was him yelling at me because he thought I was telling friends that he had COVID and he did not want anyone to know.

I did not understand why, if he were sick, he would not want help. Now I realize that if not for his ego, privacy, and secrecy, things might have been different, and maybe he could have gotten treatment sooner. If he had just let people know and had let doctors or medicine help, what could have happened? I am saddened to think what would have happened if he had just asked for help. Have you ever thought about that or let your own ego get in the way of your own success?

Oscar then said, "I found him at his house, and he had fallen, and I took him to the hospital. His wife is there as well. They are both in the ICU in the COVID ward." He continued, "I just think someone from his own family needs to be here. I am happy to help, but I thought you should know."

I immediately called my sister, Grace, and told her what Oscar had said. As we pulled up to my house, I got out of the car and walked inside. I walked up to Merrick and just lost it. I cried and cried. Why was he in the hospital? Why was he so stubborn? Why had he yelled at me and been so angry when maybe we could have helped? There are so many whys. I think that is the hardest thing to face when things are not in your control, but you try to look back to see what you could have done differently. Sometimes you really could not have done anything differently, because you were not in control. Coming to peace with that is hard.

Grace said she could leave the next morning and could fly to Orlando and assess the situation and see if she thought that I needed to come, and if so, I could fly there. She did not have kids, and it was easier for her to leave. I was sad, confused, and mad all at the same time.

Grace arrived in Orlando and went straight to the hospital. As she approached the first automatic door to the hospital, she immediately stood still in her tracks. She had had a bad case of COVID a few months before, and the reality of walking into a COVID ward did not fall lightly on her. She glanced over and saw the metal detector she would have to walk through and all the PPE everyone was wearing. As she approached the desk, the attendant asked for ID and spoke, "You will be the only approved family member that can visit Mr. Peters during the visiting hours, as our rules are very strict due to the virus." She handed Grace a name tag with her picture on it. They had copied it from her driver's license. Grace thought to herself, *There is no way that Sara Fay or Bethany can come here, since I am the only one allowed inside now.*

As she walked down the hallway, she approached the room, and a nurse greeted her there. "You will have to wear this gown, shoe bootie covers, pant covers, gloves, a hair net, a facemask shield, and a mouth mask." There was not a part of her body that could be exposed. She stared through the glass window of the steel door and could see Dad with an oxygen mask on. The room looked muggy, as if you could see COVID in the air. She quietly opened the door and had no idea what she was walking into—that it would be one of the last times she would see him.

Grace knew it was bad, and she knew that we needed to be there. I arrived the next day. Grace gave me her driver's license, and since we look alike, I was praying that I could pass for her at the strict check-in, as she was the only one allowed up. If there was a time to break the rules, it was now. I thought to myself, *I am walking into the COVID ward. I have Grace, Walker, and Merrick at home. Am I going to do this?*

I turned the doorknob. The room was dark and muggy, and all I could hear was the constant beeping and him breathing in and out of his face mask. It sounded and looked like something out of a movie, like E.T. when he was hooked up to the machines and was having trouble breathing. My dad looked over at me, and all I could see were his eyes. They closed as if to say, "I am relieved you are here," "How did you know I needed you?" and, "I am sorry" all at the same time. I thought to myself, *Where is the nurse? Where are the doctors? Where is the help?* There was help, but it was limited. Everyone needed help. It was a guessing game. Ride it out and you may get better, or you may not. The doctors seemed tired and over it. The ones that were left were completely beaten down. They had already been dealing with this for six months. I felt almost as bad for the doctors as I did for my father. They had to live this nightmare day in and day out. For what? To save someone else's life at the expense of their own and their families'? It truly was an act of true selflessness. After that day, I had a completely different outlook on healthcare workers. They are a different breed. Like nuns or priests, they had taken an oath and truly put others before themselves. How was that possible? I certainly could never have done that. I could take care of my own children and change their diapers, and possibly those of their friends if they needed me. But complete strangers? After homeschooling my kids through the lockdown, I thought teachers deserved it all. Now that's how I feel about healthcare workers!

I gazed back into his eyes and grabbed his hand. Through the gloves, I could feel a bit of warmth, a bit of cold, but a solid grip. He knew he was in trouble. What was he thinking? Was he thinking he would have lived differently if this was it? What would he have done the past month if this was it? Would he have opened another restaurant or visited his grandkids? I often think I would love to have gone back and have asked him these questions. In this moment, I could not. We needed to be the ones filled with hope. We could not ask him any of these questions, because of course we wanted to hope for and believed in the best. He also had a breathing mask on, so a long conversation would not have been possible. But I knew his thoughts were there. I could see his mind racing. He had time in that dark room to reflect on his life, to be scared, to think about what he would have done differently. That makes me sad.

Have you ever thought about that? I think naturally when we think of dying, we think of falling asleep next to the person you love in your nineties after a night of playing cards by the fire so peacefully, and life's passing is perfect. We think of a full life, even if we do not have it now. There is always "still time." But is there? How would you live your life differently if you knew it was your last few days? If you had time in a dark room to sit with your thoughts, who would you call? Who would you apologize to? What are you obsessing about today that would not matter at all in that moment? Make a list. What is important? What is important to you? What is taking up the most time in your calendar, and is that something you would be focused on lying in that dark room? Are you leaving margin in your life for what is important, margin for if your friend calls and wants to go on a walk, if your kids call and are sick and need you? Think about that. It hit hard for me and my life to the point that I had to completely shift gears. I had no margin.

I had to leave Orlando because I had an event back in South Texas. I always had an event. The dates were usually picked a year in advance, and it was happening more and more that when the dates came around, they were at the most inopportune time. My father was now on a ventilator, and my sisters were there with him. There wasn't anything I could really do at this point, and I needed to get back to work and take care of my responsibilities.

Three days later, I woke up Sunday morning, September 5, 2021. The event had been a huge success. Somehow, I was able to compartmentalize and focus on the event details and executing them. I had to put what was happening in a box in my head, because if I let myself go there, I would crumble.

Thankfully one of my friends had come to assist for the weekend and was driving. We were starving, as we had worked until 2:00 a.m. In a small country town in South Texas, there was not much to eat. We found a fried chicken stop and pulled over. As Whitney pulled into the parking spot, my phone rang, and it was my sister, Grace. She had been on top of everything: doctors, the hospital, and my dad's care. I answered the phone quickly with "Hey." She said, "I have Dad's lead nurse on the phone and am going to merge her into our call." Grace then said, "Are we all here? OK, we need to make some decisions."

The nurse began to speak: "This is what will happen if he stays on a ventilator. His body will become septic. His heart will stop, and we will have to bring in the electric shock pads. That may work for a few hours, but then he will become septic and will pass. There is no good way out of this. Either you can keep him on the ventilator for a few weeks and that will happen, or you can unplug the machine, and he should pass away peacefully in about three hours."

As I looked up at the fried chicken sign, I thought to myself, *Why am I here? How did I get here? How is this the decision that we must make today?* I noticed the sign had one bulb out. I was so sad in that moment—just deeply sad.

Chapter Two: Shifting Gears to Overcome Challenges

Whitney and Christine came back outside with the chicken biscuits and asked if I was OK. I really couldn't speak. We had told the nurse we would talk as sisters and would call her back. Driving along the two-lane road, staring out the window at the fields, I noticed a family of deer—two larger ones and smaller babies. *Is this it?* I thought. *The circle of life closes that quickly?* I thought about all the things my father had been focused on: work, restaurants, opening new concepts, burning the candle at both ends. What was he trying to prove? Who was he trying to make happy? Was he happy? He didn't seem to be to me. That made me sad. What was it all for? And how was it ending so soon at sixty-five? What was he wanting to accomplish in the next few years? Would he have spent more time with his grandkids if he knew today was his last day on earth? Why do we never think about life this way until we are dying? Have you ever thought how you would live differently if you had five years left to live? In my dad's case, it was three weeks. And during those three weeks, he was in the hospital. He had no warning. He did not have any warning that he would have five years to live so he could decide to change his life.

My mom's mother and my namesake, Fay, suddenly died in a car accident before I was born. I often think about all the things that I go through as a mother, and my immediate reaction is to call my mom. The idea that she was never able to do that as a mother is so sad to me. But she never showed it. She could have been hurting inside, but she never let a drop of rain from her own storm fall on us.

I snapped back to reality and the reality that my sisters and I had a decision to make. While we did not want to let go, we did not want him to suffer. I needed to hear again that there was zero chance in survival. If there was zero chance, I could be selfless. But if there was a chance, I could never forgive myself if we gave up.

We called the nurse back, and I said, "If we keep him on the ventilator, is there a chance of survival?" She said, "His kidneys have already failed; one by one, his other organs are starting to shut down. I cannot tell you what to do, but if it were my father, I would pull the plug. He is not there anymore. You would not be keeping him here for him; you would be keeping him here for you."

Motherhood was probably the first lesson that I had in being selfless. There is no way to truly be selfless until you have kids. It is not your fault; you just have always lived for yourself. The thought of him lying there in that room suffering was haunting. If we had the power to take him out of this pain, then we had to do so. I just could not believe it was this quick. I could not believe last night, I was orchestrating a big-name entertainer, and my biggest worry was where his tour bus could park, and now today, I was making a life-or-death decision.

The three of us called the nurse back for the third time and said the words. We said, "Go ahead and take him off the ventilator." She said, "You are doing the best thing for him. I will call you and let you know when he has passed. It will most likely be three to four hours, but sometimes, it is longer." We sobbed and sobbed and hung up the phone. I turned on his favorite Van Morrison song and stared out the window as tears rolled down my face. I was just so sad. Fifteen minutes later, the phone rang. It was the nurse. She said, "He passed away."

"What? But you said a few hours."

She said, "This means he was in even worse shape than we thought. His body was trying to shut down so badly, and now he is at peace."

While this should have given us some confirmation in our decision, it was still so hard to hear, because now it was real.

I got home, and my sisters and I sat in the family room on the sofa. We decided we just needed to sit in our grief, cry, and listen to Van Morrison. We were not ready for the world to know the news yet. So many people loved him, and he had made a difference in so many lives. But we needed our time before the frenzy ensued.

My phone rang, and it was my mom. She had begun getting calls that the news was out. What? How did people know? We just needed a few hours alone, a few hours to cry and be sad.

My phone rang again; it was a 901 number. "Hello?" On the other end, I heard a woman's voice say, "Hi, is this Sara Fay, Tommy Peters's daughter?"

"Yes, it is."

"This is Michelle from NBC 5 in Memphis; I am sorry for your loss. Can you tell me what impact the loss of your father will have on the city of Memphis?" What? I had not had a chance to even tell family members, and the news station was already calling. OK, switch gears. Put on my event face and go.

I had been in communication with many of the Beale Street Blues Company employees over the past few weeks as the power of attorney, making decisions while Tommy was on the ventilator. But I thought that was temporary. I was just trying to make the best decisions that I could, make the decisions that I thought he would make based on the facts that I had, which I knew were not all the facts. Big decisions were thrown at me. "Sara Fay, B. B. King's New Orleans is set to reopen after COVID on September 15. Do you want to reopen the restaurant?" ... "Sara Fay, your father has a contract out to open a recording studio; can you sign it?" ... "Sara Fay, your father is supposed to be in Vegas tomorrow to testify in a trial; can you be there in his place?" ... "Sara Fay, we need your comment on a lawsuit in Orlando; what is your position?" ... "Sara Fay, Sara Fay, Sara Fay," from all directions.

If I had thought about all these things at once, I would have crumbled! I had to take a decision at a time with only the facts I had in front of me. *Do not let yourself get overwhelmed. This is a big thing,* I told myself. *You can do it.*

The car pulled into my driveway after the long drive home. I needed to sit in the quiet. I needed to be with my sisters, listen to Van Morrison, process what had happened, and cry.

We had only been home about thirty minutes, and the checklist started inside my head. I needed to write a PR statement and communicate the truth to employees. Many of them had been with my father for years and years. Some of them knew him better than I did. They needed someone to tell them the news, comfort them in their time of grief, tell them they still had a job, and tell them it was going to be OK, all at the same time. *OK, I can do this. Fake it until you make it, Sara Fay. Be authentic, be yourself, and it will be OK.*

My life had completely changed. I did not even know yet all the ways it would change. Why me? I already have so much on my plate, so why me? I could not see the positive through the darkness yet.

Even though I did not realize this was my future yet, something was enticing. Something was calling me to "fix it." Something was exciting about the mess. Many times, we are thrown a situation that is a mess. It is not in any way because of our own doing, but we look up, and now it is our mess to clean up. It is what we do with that mess that matters, the people in that mess. How will you let your mess define you? You can curl up and cry, get overwhelmed by the anxiety of it all for sure. And there are definitely days like that. Tequila also helps! But take a step back for a second.

Chapter Two Takeaways and Reflections

#1: The Mess

What are the messes in your life?

- Write them down.

  _____
  _____
  _____
  _____

- Does any part of these messes bring you joy or excitement? If the answer is yes, write down how you can figure out a way to work through this situation to better your life on the other side of it.

  _____
  _____
  _____
  _____

- If the answer is no, then the mess is a completely dark hole, so move on!

I have learned through the spiderweb of situations that so many of them are not fair. I did not have anything to do with many of these messes, but I inherited them.

#2: Money and Fairness

Money. Money is a mess. Have you noticed what money does to people? Don't do anything just because of the money. Do it because you love it, because you believe in it and are passionate about it, and the money will come. You can always tell when someone is driven by money, and it usually backfires.

If I think about the money and the money that I have lost, I will get so wrapped up in the negative that I literally could not move forward. Instead, I think about the people, the people and the facts about the situation in front of me, and I let that drive my decision. That has worked for me. I have had to walk away from situations where it would have been easy to file a lawsuit or fight and fight for what I thought was right. But where would that get me in the end? Would I be happier? Probably not. The situation still would have happened. Would I feel rightly rewarded in the end? Probably not. The lawyers would have been the only ones properly rewarded.

#3: Letting Go

It is hard to walk away. Think about it. Is there anyone in your life that when you see their name light up on your phone, anxiety runs through your veins? I have had those people, and usually I do not realize it until it is too late.

- Are there any situations that are weighing on you? What are they?

  _____
  _____
  _____
  _____

- What can you do today to remove those people and those situations from your life?

  _____
  _____
  _____
  _____

They carry a black cloud that hovers over you even if you do not realize it, and it is holding you back. While it may not be fair, it is holding you back from being the best you. Future opportunities that could bring more joy to your life are waiting for you.

Say goodbye to those situations; let them go. The choice is yours. You are the only person in control of your life! What if you got the call tomorrow about only living for five more years?

- How would you live differently?

  _____
  _____
  _____
  _____

- What changes would you make with the people and situations in your life?

  _____
  _____
  _____
  _____

Reflecting on the key moments where my life shifted gears, I had it all on paper: a dream event-planning career that took me across the world to other countries to plan dreamlike weddings fit for *Vogue*, making every bride jealous on Instagram. I look up now three years after my father passed away, and I reflect on the messiness of the past three years—the storms, the challenge—and I wouldn't change a thing. I know if those storms would not have happened, I would not be where I am today. I sit here today in really deep happiness. I look at my husband and hug him tight. I look at my kids and think of simple moments as our last and truly cherish them.

I wasn't that person before.

I look at my house filled with kids running around carrying mud through the carpet, and I do not care. This is what it is all about: the messiness, the house full of love, people, food, and laughter. I know now these days are short-lived, and I do not want to miss a moment.

Chapter Three

CULTIVATING HUMAN CONNECTION

The Significance of Genuine Connections and the Positive Effects They Have on Individuals

As we let our own light shine, we unconsciously give other people permission to do the same. As we are liberated from our fear, our presence automatically liberates others.

—MARIANNE WILLIAMSON

Where do you even start with forming deep, genuine connections with people? I truly believe you must be in the right headspace to let people in and to truly listen in order to make that connection. So, what do you do first? Unplug yourself!

I am a huge believer in this, especially being in an industry in which you always have to be ON. It is important to take time for yourself. Whether it is travel, reading a book, or watching a mindless TV show, everyone needs to reset. The people that burn the candle at both ends just end up being burned out. You will only be better for yourself, your family, your company, and your team when you take the time to reset.

The Italian philosophy of *dolce far niente*, the sweetness of doing nothing, was a lesson I embraced while basking in the Saturday sun beside the azure waters of Lake Como. Turning off the work brain was a revelation, a baptism in the art of leisure. This act of self-care isn't just a respite; it's a recharge, a necessary pause that fortifies us for the journey ahead.

I used to think that this meant you were not a hard worker. As an American, I have this sense that I always felt like I could not put the "out of office" notification on. I had to always be available to be the best that I could be in my career. As I have gotten older, I have realized that it's actually the opposite. It is OK to take time for yourself. Now that mental health is getting more and more awareness, it is getting easier to take a vacation or a break. But the Italians have this down to a science. They take a month off in the summer and take a lunch break every day and have no qualms about it. Their thought process is very matter-of-fact about it, and no one questions it, because it is what it is.

"Can you please send me a wedding proposal for a wedding next May in Ravello? I am meeting with the bride in a month."

"Nope, sorry! I am leaving on holiday for the off season for four months and will get back to you when I get back. But do not worry, everything will be great!"

And you know what? It probably would be. Why do I stress so much? I realized I needed to be in the moment more and be present.

I truly believe you need to take a break and take care of yourself first before you can really relax and form the personal connection with others that is needed. You must let that inner checklist in your brain stop so you can look people in the eyes and truly listen.

Chapter Three: Cultivating Human Connection

Out of Office

Some of my favorite clients I have met while traveling. My husband and I were on our fifteen-year anniversary trip in Lake Como. My mind is always looking around at the hospitality side, no matter where I am! "Oh, that lawn would be gorgeous for a wedding ceremony. Oh, that would make the cutest bar façade!" I cannot help but analyze all the serving pieces at the bars and restaurants and consider how to incorporate it into an event or restaurant. I love to travel. I think traveling and experiencing different cultures and hospitality in different countries opens our eyes to so much more.

It was a Saturday in June, and Merrick and I were in the pool in Lake Como. What? Pinch me! First, it is a Saturday. I feel like a bride on her honeymoon. Usually, I am schlepping underneath tables on a Saturday and not the one laying out enjoying the sun. I almost did not know how to relax. It was the first day, and I always have a hard time turning my "go, go" work brain off. But we were in such a beautiful place, and I knew I had to stop thinking about my next wedding and my to-do list running through my head and try to turn off my work brain to relax and enjoy this gorgeous part of Italy.

I looked over across the pool and saw the most striking mother-daughter trio. They were stunning and clearly American, dressed head to toe in the most beautiful designer bathing suits, cover-ups, huge sunglasses, and handbags. I needed to know their story. I absolutely love people-watching. And then I heard their Southern accents and a mention of Jimmy Choo stilettos, and I knew we were in good company. Turning off my ongoing to-do list in my brain allowed me to genuinely look them in the eye and form a connection that would last to this day. The ultimate through line!

I saw the girls go toward the hot tub. I wanted to know more and meet them. I put down my book on the lounge chair, adjusted my hat and sunglasses, and started to walk over. I dipped my first toe into the hot tub and saw they were looking me over. "I love your entire look! Where are you from?" I started. Treasure immediately said, "We are from Texas, but I live in New York City." They had a glimmer in their eye about all three of them that made me want to know more about their story. I smiled and waved over to the server, dressed in a full khaki suit, watching the bright sun gleam on this forehead, and said, "*Signore*, please bring us and my new friends a bottle of your favorite Vermentino!" Nothing like a nice glass of Italian white wine to bring people together! I'm not sure why, but I would have never done this in Dallas. I would be too busy. I would be on to the next thing on my to-do list. Why did it take me going to another country to disconnect from my own emails, calls, and to-do list and connect with others?

We quickly learned that one of the daughters had recently called off her wedding, and the two sisters and her mother had had a rough year with her father undergoing chemotherapy treatment for cancer. Looking into their eyes, I saw a glimmer of joy and the deep love of being with one another. I also sensed a collective sadness, even though we were in one of the most magical settings in the world. You can always tell by someone's eyes what is really happening deep down. My authentic conversations that day with these complete strangers really stuck with me. You really never know what is going on with someone else until you ask. So many assumptions are made today by just looking at someone—what they are wearing, what they drive, how they look. This is what we are teaching our kids through social media. I encourage you to dive into your friendships. Ask the hard questions. You may be frustrated with someone in your life, but you may not have the full picture. Don't jump to judgements and conclusions. Just ask first.

Chapter Three: Cultivating Human Connection

My heart broke for these girls, and little did I know what heartbreak was in store for me soon after this trip. It turned out we had the same itinerary and ended up at the same hotel together, Splendido in Portofino.

Our first night there, we were soon dancing on the piano together, belting out "Dancing Queen" like we were long-lost friends. Several late-night piano bar and champagne conversations led to one of the sisters telling me that when she got married next time, she would call me to plan her wedding. And she did, two years later!

It is a small world. Being yourself and opening up in an authentic way can lead to friendships or even working together in ways you wouldn't imagine. This particular through line of life wove together in the most unexpected way.

It's interesting, but every wedding client I ever had was from word of mouth or friends of friends. This is the best and most soulful and authentic way to grow your business.

Another mother of the bride I met while flying on an airplane. She was seated next to me on American Airlines, flying to Jacksonville, Florida. We ended up talking the entire way. Her eyes had such a genuine kindness about her that I felt like I could learn something from her. She asked me about my wedding business, and I asked her about her life. I usually am not this type of person. I usually am on an airplane with headphones on, laptop out, and loving every minute because my phone isn't ringing! Airplane rides are my most productive hours! But this day was different. I felt as if our paths would cross again, but I did not know how or where or the end of this story. She called me months later to tell me her daughter was engaged, and she would love for me to fly to Colorado to plan her daughter's wedding. She had not seen any of my work and did not have any references, but the connection we made that day on that plane formed a trust that not only led to a friendship but a beautiful and special wedding.

These interactions have taught me that you must open your eyes and look around. Take chances to connect with someone, wherever you find yourself. The wedding was magical! But I know you are also here for the juicy funny stories, and I would be remiss if I did not tell you one hilarious story from this wedding! Let's take a break and laugh!

You Wouldn't Believe

It was 2:00 p.m. in Cordillera, Colorado, the day of the wedding. Everything was going as planned. It was June, and the wildflowers were blooming on the mountain, and the sun was out, the perfect weather for a summer mountain wedding. The wedding cake had arrived, and we had just finished putting the flower topper on the top layer. The cake sat on a round table in the center of the open-air tent off the back of the club house. Now that the tent setup was finished, I could focus on the inside of the club. I walked inside, and as I looked back outside the glass window, I saw something black moving and coming toward the tent. What was that? Was I going crazy? As the black figure came closer, we realized it was a bear! "Aah! Get inside, everyone!" The bear was very happy, and nothing was stopping him. He strolled right up to that wedding cake and took a swipe with his hands. Realizing it was food, he began eating the entire cake until it was completely melted icing.

Oh my goodness, I thought to myself. *Did that really just happen?* At least it was not during the wedding, and we still had an hour to get another cake. But we were in the mountains, not a city! I called the cake lady, and thankfully, she had the cake for the next weekend's wedding in the freezer. It was completely frozen and a different design, but it was white and would have to do!

Later that night, when it was time for the bride to cut the cake, she said, "It's frozen and won't cut." And I said, "Just smile for the picture, and I'll tell you all about it tomorrow!"

The Business of Being Yourself Helps You to Connect

True connection in business is a mirror of personal authenticity. Through encounters by poolsides or on airplanes, treating every individual as a valued future client has proven to be the cornerstone of my career. This genuine approach has turned strangers into clients and clients into lifelong friends, reinforcing the belief that one's own personality is their most invaluable and unique asset.

In the crystal waters of Lake Como, I found a reflection of life's unpredictability. A chance encounter with this mother-daughter trio unfolded an experience of shared humanity—a tale of love, loss, and the resilience of the human spirit. Our paths, crossing by chance, led to a synchronicity of experiences, from the luxurious tranquility of Lake Como to the historic elegance of Portofino, where the rhythm of "Dancing Queen" bound us in a dance of newfound friendship and future promises! Be yourself, and business will follow! Don't focus too hard on sales but more on the relationships you are forming.

- How can you weave your inner self into your business? That will create sales!

  _____
  _____
  _____
  _____
  _____

- What do you have that is unique and special that you can bring to the table?

  _____
  _____
  _____
  _____
  _____

- What does your business have that is unique and special that it can bring to the table?

  _____
  _____
  _____
  _____
  _____

> **PRO TIP**
>
> *My secret to a successful business: I simply get to know the client, spending nights, meals, weekends together. Throw away the Pinterest pages. Yes, that can give you an idea of what their taste is, but to really get something authentic, I look in their closet, go to their home, see how they live, see where they eat, ask about their travels. Infusing all their favorite experiences throughout the wedding or event is always my approach.*

Chameleon Sales

I originally learned the concept of chameleon sales from Todd Fiscus, my first boss. Have you heard of this concept? Just as chameleons change their color to be like that of their environment, you must adapt to your surroundings to make your client feel more comfortable. For example, if you are selling something—anything really—and sitting across from you in the room is a woman covered in sequins, just naturally learn to rise to their level of excitement or energy. Or the opposite: if they're very, very soft-spoken, you try to meet them where they are. And then in doing so, you also meet them on a different level of connecting with them. Bring your voice to high or low depending on where they are; watch their body language and what they are doing with their hands. Dress appropriately. I always want the person that I am meeting to feel comfortable with me. I want to always be myself and show my own style, but also make them feel comfortable at the same time. If I am going into a corporate office, I may have on a suit, but if I am going to someone's home, I would wear black pants and a blouse. Professional yet comfortable in someone's home is key. This is a subtle trick that helps the person you are meeting with put down the wall that they may have up when you first walk in. Then you can have a natural exchange of energy and conversation and hopefully connect in a much faster, deeper, and natural way.

Eye Contact

When Grace was in the hospital, we had to all wear masks because of the COVID rules and regulations. The funny thing about wearing a mask is it forces you to look at people's eyes. You do not need to see the rest of their face most of the time, the eyes tell you everything you need to know. I did not realize how important eye contact was until I went through these life-or-death situations with a mask on. I realized that the eyes of everyone I spoke to told me everything I needed to know about them in that moment. The very fact that I was forced to only look at their eyes just opened a whole new way of looking at human interaction, a new way of communication.

It's the People!

What I love about events, weddings, and restaurants are all the same things. It is all the same through line. I love knowing that when you talk to people, really talk to people, everyone has something going on in their life. You are not the only one with drama, with family issues, with health issues, with work issues.

But being in the hospitality space, we have the true privilege of creating a space, an atmosphere, a climate to take the guests and customers out of their life for a few hours, to transport them to another place, a place where if the music is just right, the food is just right, the lighting is just right, and the drinks hit just right, then they can escape. This place they are transported to helps them to forget all their worries for just a few hours, and they can be whoever they want to be in that moment. Now that is a privilege. That is something special.

I think people were surprised to hear that I went from planning very high-end weddings to managing blues clubs and restaurants, but to me, it is all the same. It is all about the people—the people who work so hard to make this atmosphere, music, and food so special, and the people that walk through the doors that allow us to do what we do. These people are everything. Without the people, it wouldn't be possible with any business.

In both event planning and restaurants, I have found that if you put the people first over money with your decision making, the money will come. When you make smart decisions with your heart and pour your authenticity into your business and your people, the money will come.

Get to know people, their families, their dynamics, and how they interact with each other. Learn chameleon sales. Find a common ground with the person in front of you and go off that, even if they do not have the same taste as you. Try to put yourself in their shoes. Then you can actually get excited about the project. Take what they want, and put a beautiful and tasteful spin on it. That is what makes a true artist—being able to take what the client wants and make it beautiful no matter the style. It's fun and it is a challenge, and it keeps it interesting. There's never a dull moment when you have fun with your job and the task at hand!

Connection Tips and Advice

- Collect friends—all kinds of friends! The most fun parties are when everyone isn't the same.

- Live right in the mess. It can be perfect, happy, and beautiful. Don't listen to or worry about what others say about what you are doing. Just go for it!

- It doesn't matter what you are selling; there are through lines everywhere. Just look for them, and just continue looking for them.

- Treat everyone the same. Everyone you encounter is a future client, with any industry you are in, and especially hospitality. It may not be the exact person you are interacting with, but their best friend may be your best future client. In the restaurant business certainly, everyone is your customer. You are your best calling card.

- You are in control of the one thing that no one else can top you on. That is your own personality.

- When nothing is beneath you, everything goes for you!

- Be authentic!

- Find something to love about a client or customer even though you want to spit in their soup.

- Ask the questions, have the conversations, and really

listen! Do you ever ask a question and then realize that you are not paying attention to the answer?

- Think about your response before you answer. Are they asking for advice from you or just for someone to listen?

- Mean it. When you really listen to what the other person is saying and stop thinking about your own story—how you are going to share when they finish their sentence and one-up their story. Then you actually start caring and the real authenticity happens.

Making a Getaway

I have driven many departure cars away. Was that the smartest thing to do? Did I have the correct insurance? Was I willing to do anything to make the client happy? No, no, and *yes*! And I did it with a smile because I genuinely loved it, actually smiled and laughed the whole way.

One of my absolute favorite brides and dear friends to this day was someone in a departure car. We got to know each other really well on the ride home. Her wedding was in Marfa, Texas, at the chic Thunderbird Hotel. The getaway car was her father's hunting jeep in full West Texas style. I kept asking through the planning process, "Who is going to drive the jeep to your honeymoon house?" She would say, "Oh, my uncle is the only one that can drive it; do not worry, it will be fine!" I had a bad feeling about this. Of course I worried, as that was what I was hired to do: worry about every possible thing that could go wrong. But I always seemed to worry a little about the thing that I knew wasn't completely checked off my checklist!

That night, as I suspected, her favorite uncle had so much fun at the reception that he was not the best person to drive the bride and groom home. Well, nothing like hiking up my black dress and trying to remember how to drive a stick shift from my one-time, thirty-year-ago lesson. But this would be an adventure!

They were giddy in the back seat as I jerked the gears side to side. I can always tell, and I always have my hunch while watching the bride and groom, and these two were lovebirds for life!

I had no idea where I was going, and it was completely dark. There were no streetlights, everything was closed at midnight, and it was only us on the road. Even the once-flashing Thunderbird neon sign was dark. The bride said, "Just follow the road down to the water tower, and when you see the water tower, turn on the dirt road to the right, and there will be the house we rented." I just kept driving. As I saw the water tower and turned back, the two lovebirds were … having a moment. They were the cutest, and I did not want to interrupt. *Did I get paid enough for this?* I thought to myself. *Ha, but it will be the best story!* I turned right at the water tower, and no house. I turned left, and no house. I finally found the house and honked loudly to bring them back to reality and let them know we had arrived. To this day, we still joke about me driving their honeymoon car. A can-do attitude, a smile, a yes, a connection may not always be the smartest decision, but it usually will get you a great story and a real friend in the end!

As I remember the laughter-filled drive in that West Texas hunting jeep, transporting a jubilant bride and groom, I realize that these are the moments that define us. A willingness to embrace the unexpected, to dive into the moment with heart and soul, creates memories that linger and relationships that endure. This is the art of connection—messy, unpredictable, but oh so beautiful. To this day, we are still great friends and actually worked together in business.

Chapter Three Takeaways and Reflections

This chapter has journeyed through the landscape of human connection, from the spark of eye contact to the depths of shared experiences. We've seen how authenticity, a pause from the grind, and the embrace of serendipity can enrich our lives and businesses. The essence lies in being present, being real, and valuing every person as a piece of a larger, beautiful puzzle.

- What steps can you take today to stop, breathe, and recharge?

  _____

  _____

  _____

- What can you put on your calendar now for pauses over the next month, six months, and year to set aside time for you to recharge?
  - **This week** (Ex: Go for a walk.):

    _____

    _____

    _____

- ☐ **This month** *(Ex: Plan dinner with a friend that fills your cup.)*:

  _____
  _____
  _____

- ☐ **Next six months** *(Ex: Cut something off your calendar that does not bring you joy.)*:

  _____
  _____
  _____

- ☐ **This year** *(Ex: Plan a trip to somewhere that makes you happy with your favorite person.)*:

  _____
  _____
  _____

• What is a recent experience you had that, if you had smiled and laughed through it instead of stressed through it, could have had a different internal outcome for you?

_____
_____
_____

Chapter Three: Cultivating Human Connection

Remember what to do when a situation arises, and you do not know how to handle it. First, stop, breathe, and think of a road map in your head before you act. How can your actions change others' actions or attitudes in this scenario? How can you lead with a positive attitude through the situation?

Chapter Four

WHENEVER POSSIBLE, HAVE A BACKUP PLAN

Success Often Depends on Whether You're Ready with a Backup Plan, Because Things Rarely—If Ever—Go as Planned

My little Texas tornado, blowing me away again. I swore it wouldn't happen again.

—TRACY LAWRENCE

In life and business, success often hinges on having a solid backup plan, as experience has taught me things rarely go as planned.

It was a Thursday in March, and the tip of my boot was crunching through the knee-high tumbleweeds as I walked through a field in Weatherford, Texas. The sun was beaming. It was such a beautiful day and was going to be a gorgeous weekend for a ranch wedding. The bride was Treasure, the woman who I met three years before in Lake Como with Merrick. She was engaged to the cutest real-life cowboy, and she kept her promise and called me to plan the wedding! It made it even more special to work with someone that I had already shared a special connection with. I wanted everything to be perfect for her!

I had already made my decision that this was going to be one of my last weddings to plan. This was because the stresses over the past twenty years of being gone every weekend, missing kids' games and special moments, had all gotten to be too much. Then it intensified with the passing of my father, my daughter's illness, and running the restaurants. Enough was enough. I couldn't do this anymore. I couldn't be everything for everyone. But God knows I loved planning weddings. As I walked through that field, I thought to myself, *I am good at this. I love this, and I am good at this.* To do something that you truly love and feel good at it is a blessing. Not many people can say that.

The tables, chairs, sofas, stage, and dance floor were already set up. It looked like we could have the wedding that night! The two custom tents had been going up for two straight weeks. The clear plexiglass walls, wood floor, and chandeliers full of greenery were all so chic and were going to be the perfect combination of "New York fashion meets Texas ranch" for the New York–loving, PR-mogul bride and the cowboy groom. It was so them, which was always my goal! There was not going to be one flower in the entire wedding. It would be so unique and so vogue! The tables were going to be set with thousands of clear glasses and floating candles. Instead of flowers on the tables, we created custom chandeliers to hang over each table with cascading greenery the exact length of the tables. It was going to be so incredible and at night would put off the most incredible glow, sitting in the middle of the empty pasture.

That night I was driving back to Dallas, thinking to myself, *Should I be stepping back from weddings? I love this so much, and I am good at it! Maybe I can do it all?* As I walked into the house, the channel five news was on, and the kids were crowded around the TV in the family room. "Mom, there is a tornado coming! Should we get in the closet, or can I still watch the Stars game?" shouted Walker. I heard the voice of David Finfrock come over the airways. He was warning of tornadoes coming later that night. It sounded like it would be west of us, and as long as it steered clear of my tent, we would be fine. *What are the chances?* "No, sweetie, we are fine; the warnings are not near us now. Let's make dinner. Do not worry!" I assured him.

The next morning, the news showed a tractor trailer turned over at the exact exit where we turned to go to the ranch where the wedding tent was. I called the owner of the ranch, and he said, "I cannot leave my house, but I can see the tent in the distance, and it still looks like it is standing!" Well, that was good news. I drove as fast as I could to the tent site. The drive from Dallas to Weatherford was uneventful. As I got three exits out from my turn, I noticed the street signs were gone. The billboards were blown away. This was not a good sign.

As I parked and walked up to the mangled tent, I could not believe what I saw. "In forty years, I have never, ever seen this happen!" said Mike Sandone, who owned the tent company. He said, "Lightning struck the tent, and that is why the metal is sizzled in half!" I felt a pit in my stomach. How was it possible that the craziest things continued to happen? Just when I thought I had seen it all and everything possible had happened to a wedding, a tornado hits it, and literally hits the exact tent out of all of Texas! I was so cocky the day before, singing and patting myself on the back. Was this God trying to hit me over the head to say, "Yes, Sara Fay, it is time"? I think so! He was saying, bring yourself back down to earth, and if you won't listen to me, I will remind you who is in charge!

With the help of some amazing vendors, somehow, we took apart the broken and fractured tent and hauled it away. And though it had taken two weeks to install, we managed to put up a new tent in twenty-four hours. By Saturday afternoon, just in time, the tent was ready for the bride and her family, and not a minute earlier. She did not know what had happened to the tent that Thursday night. I did not want that to be the drama of her weekend and literally steal her thunder! She deserved to be the star! I told her after the wedding and started a shared photo album called "Texas Tornado." It was time for me to hang that wedding cowgirl hat up for good this time!

My Support System

In this case, the backup plan was my support system—the people around me that I had formed relationships with over many years. I have been there for them, so they were going to be there for me. Surrounding yourself with the right people is everything. Life is all about relationships.

Sometimes there are at least four or more backup plans for events. For a tented wedding, I usually lay out in advance as many as possible for all foreseeable situations.

For example:

- Plan A: Light rain in the forecast could mean we need a tent covering with no walls.
- Plan B: Sideways rain in the forecast could mean we need more tents with side walls, additional generators, air-conditioning, walkways, and staff with umbrellas, which all really affects the budget last minute.
- Plan C: A tornado, which means think of safety and your guests first and have a safe place for guests and staff to go for protection.
- Plan D: The tornado hits the tent, and you call in *all* favors from all the vendors and people you have formed relationships

with over the years. And because of those connections, they will usually step in and go above and beyond to support you at all costs, pulling off the unthinkable at times.
- In all plans, you have to trust both your support system but also your instincts and your inner gut.

> **What did I learn from this experience, and what can you learn from it?**
> - Listen to that inner voice inside of you!
> - Don't pat yourself on the back until the fat lady sings or your task is completely over; there is always still work to do!
> - Getting too comfortable in your position can get your mind off what you need to still be focused on!
> - You can be good at things and not do them. It is OK.
> - You cannot be everything for everybody. You must take care of yourself first!
> - Surround yourself with people you trust and who have your back! This wedding would have never been pulled off without me surrounding myself with amazing vendors who worked to make it happen.
> - Sometimes your backup plan is the people around you! Lift them up constantly so they will always support you, even in a tornado!

I have always said, when you have the best backup plans and rain plans, you do not need them.

the THROUGH *line*

One for the Books—or in This Case, My Book!

It was another wedding that our team thought we had all figured out! Our entire team took bets on if the bride would show up on the wedding day. Everyone concluded there was about a 0.007 percent chance that she would show. So we needed the most foolproof, ironclad, least-embarrassing plan B there could possibly be.

A little background on why we felt so strongly about this: most of our meetings would go like this. The bride's personal assistant would send us a rider before each meeting. A rider is a term used by a performer for a list of items required for their performance, such as lighting, sound system, power, water, sweat towels, food, etc. Never in my life had a client sent a list of their preferred requests for a meeting! The rider was fantastic and read as such:

> Regardless of time of each meeting with the client. It is in your best interest to provide the following to be set and ready for each appointment.
>
> - A standing cocktail table outside the front door with an ashtray, various British tabloids such as *The Mirror, The Sun,* or the *Daily Mail.*
>
> - An ice-cold dog bowl of water for her dog and a dog leash in case she does not have one.
>
> - Set inside the meeting at arm's length, a bottle of Macallan 12 single malt scotch for the groom, a few bottles of Far Niente Chardonnay for the bride and various salty snacks

After this first request, I absolutely could not wait to meet the couple. A dark Mercedes-Maybach pulled into the parking lot, and the driver, clad in a black tuxedo and black driving cap, opened the door as the tall, slender bride took a step out of the car and lankily approached us. Her sunglasses were oversized and covered two thirds of her face. Something was off. Had she already been drinking? It was 10:38 a.m., and she had an unlit cigarette dangling from her mouth as if she forgot it was there. I immediately was mesmerized! This was going to be fun! She quickly explained she had just come from a quick liposuction procedure where the doctor had taken just a bit of fat from her buttock and injected it in her lips. That explained her not being able to feel the cigarette on her plump lips.

One of the first items on the agenda was that the groom needed groomsmen. The groom did not have too many prospects himself, so we needed to schedule a modeling audition. *This job just gets more fun by the minute,* I thought!

I was so excited for the audition day that I pulled up to the client's house a little early. It was a quarter to ten in the morning; the groom stopped me outside as he approached his green Aston Martin. He slurred, "Heeeeyyyyy, wedding planner!" His clothes appeared wrinkled, as if he was wearing the clothes from the night before, and his face was bright-red with splotches. "Can you do me a favor and just blow into this hose for me to the left of my steering wheel?" I thought for a second. You really could never make up a job description for this job! I did not know what to do.

I was in a state of shock, as I was confused why he would be leaving and would not want to interview his own groomsmen, while at the same time trying to decide if this was really a breathalyzer! I mean, I was the hired help, and the people pleaser in me looked at him and held the tube and blew. He quickly drove off and I immediately felt a huge sense of guilt. Did that just happen? What if he got into an accident and someone was hurt? It would be my fault he was driving. One of the assistants hurried outside to call me to come inside, and I looked at her in disbelief. I told her what had just happened, and she said, "Oh don't worry! He does this every day, and he will have to blow again at every stoplight, so don't feel too bad. Now come inside and let's get to work."

We hired eight male models that day and had them fitted for tuxedos to stand by the groom on his wedding day. The bride was all set, as her bridesmaids included her assistant, dog walker, stylist, hairdresser, and daughter.

I learned a lot from the planning process, but I knew we needed many backup plans to be prepared for anything that came our way.

We did not want to have the embarrassing moment for me, the wedding planner, to stand at the front of the ceremony with guests seated and the strings playing and say, "Ladies and gentlemen, there will not be a wedding today!" I had only had to do it once in my career, and I was not going to do it again if possible!

So, we planned to have a pre-ceremony cocktail hour in a beautiful grove of trees when the guests arrived. This would be lovely, with a string quartet playing and servers passing champagne. When the bride arrived at the property, fully dressed and ready to walk down the aisle, at that moment and that moment only, we would ask guests to be seated for the ceremony. It would be much less embarrassing to take guests directly from the cocktail hour to a seated dinner and just skip the whole "I do" thing if the bride didn't show.

I still want to believe that, for some reason, it was our foolproof backup plan that gave the bride the gumption to show that day! She arrived, and oh, did we have a ceremony. See, the funny part was, no one thought the bride would show, but she wanted to play a prank on the guests so they would think the groom wasn't going to show. You can't make this up!

Once the bride arrived, we kindly asked the guests to be seated. The ceremony chairs were perfectly situated in the most gorgeous garden with thousands of flowers. Orchids cascaded down the aisle as a bridge formed the walkway over a pond just before the altar area. The bride could not decide on her bouquet for the wedding day and had our floral team make forty bouquets for her to select from before she walked down the aisle. As she approached the archway at the top of the aisle and saw the row of forty bouquets lining the aisle for her selection, she threw her cigarette out of her mouth onto the dewy grass and grabbed a four-foot-long, cascading phalaenopsis white-orchid bouquet. The dog walker pressed the shock collar, prompting the yellow lab to run down the aisle with the rings as the bride took her stance at the top of the aisle.

She walked down the aisle to a full orchestra loudly sounding "Canon in D." As the bride took her first few steps toward the altar, one thing was missing: the groom!

Suddenly, the orchestra stopped, and a familiar song came across the loudspeakers. *Dun dun dun da, dun dun da … da da da … da da da … dun na …* "Is that 'Mission Impossible'?" questioned a lady in the back row with her perfectly pink summer hat. "What is that? Are we under attack?" The loud vibrations of a helicopter blade roared overhead as a midnight-gray helicopter came closer toward us.

What the guests did not know is that I was the one in the back with the walkie-talkie, orchestrating the entire scene. Thirty minutes before, when the bride was not on property and had yet to select her bouquet, the helicopter pilot had radioed me to say he only had a little over thirty minutes of gas. I had to make the helicopter entrance for the groom, or it would not happen!

As the sound of the blades came closer, the door to the helicopter opened, and a rope flung out of the cavity. A man in a black tuxedo appeared. "Whoa! Jack?" proclaimed a few guests. The guests thought it was the groom; the crazy, insane plan was working perfectly. The tuxedo-clad man gripped onto the rope and made his way down further as the helicopter hovered over the altar. The man then leapt and fell behind the hedge lining the front barrier of the ceremony. Up popped Jack, the groom! He brushed off the leaves on his lapel and skipped toward his bride.

What guests could not see was my assistant behind the bushes, who had been waiting with the groom there the entire ceremony as the groom's look-alike stunt double jumped out of the helicopter.

It was all too crazy; there was no way this plan was falling into place! At least I did not have to recite my plan B speech inviting guests straight to the dinner! Even the most elaborate plans can go off plan, but if you've got quick thinking skills and the right team, you can usually make it work!

PRO TIP

I have had two weddings involving helicopters, and both couples did not stay married long. When planning a wedding, make sure you don't lose focus that after the big day is over, that is when the big life starts. Make sure you are marrying the right person and would love them with or without the helicopter entrance. When you are with the right person, it just keeps getting better.

Chapter Four: Whenever Possible, Have a Backup Plan

When You Don't Have a Backup Plan

Over the years, one of the biggest lessons that I have learned the hard way is to always have a backup plan. I am inherently a people pleaser. I hate telling people no. I love taking their ideas and bringing what they want to life. But after years of being in business, I have learned it is OK to say no. The clients are paying you for your opinion. The ones that will not accept your opinion may not be the best fit for your business. Those clients are usually the ones that will never be happy in the end and will not remember that the plans were their ideas and not your ideas and that you tried to warn them. In the end, you will be the one stuck with the issue.

Many years ago, somewhere toward the beginning of my wedding-planning experiences, I was hungry for weddings, and I wanted all the weddings! It was early spring in Dallas, and a client called with a request. He wanted to have a wedding in fifteen days in his backyard. No problem! I could handle this. The only caveat was that he had many relationships around town and wanted to use all his own vendors: his friend the DJ, his friend that had the valet company, his friend the caterer, his friend that did wedding cakes, etc. This was not the norm. Even early on, I had vendors that I relied on and trusted. Most of the people that he wanted me to work with on the wedding I had never worked with before or heard of. Red flag number one! But what could go wrong? This wasn't a foreign country; this was Dallas, in a backyard, at home! Piece of cake!

It was the first weekend of May, and the wedding day was here. I had a new intern starting that day, and I had asked her to show up at the house. I asked her to go upstairs and be with the bride. If the bride needs anything, just help her and be with her for hair and makeup. I proceeded to greet all the vendors and set up the wedding in the backyard. It really was pretty. We had beautiful cabana tents over the food stations, bars, and dance area. I just love a backyard wedding; they are so unique and specialized to the couple. Again, what could go wrong?

Most everything was set as my new intern radioed to me on the walkie-talkie. "Sara Fay, the bride refuses to put on any clothes until she has her diamond tiara, and the tiara is locked inside the Range Rover." I said, "Do not panic; just find the keys and get the tiara for her so she can get dressed." After a long search for keys, they were nowhere to be found. At this point, guests were arriving as another person on my team radioed. "Sara Fay, we have three hundred guests arriving, and his friend, the valet, that showed up is only one person!" I quickly said, "Just start parking cars and direct guests to park the cars along the road; I am dealing with a naked bride here!"

"Sara Fay, can I have permission to throw a brick through the Range Rover window?" yelled the first-day intern.

"Yes, anything to get her to put clothes on!"

"OK, I have the brick in my hand and am about to throw …"

"Wait!" I yelled. "Is the car right next to the ceremony, and is there an alarm that will go off?"

"Shoot, yes," she said.

"Then you cannot do that. I will go talk to the bride. You run down the street to the nearest bridal boutique and buy any tiara you can find; I don't care what it looks like!"

"Sara Fay!" another voice started on the radio. "The wedding cake is melting; what do we do? We have to cut it now before the ceremony, or it will completely fall apart."

"OK, stay calm; can you get four servers on all sides of the table and move the cake inside out of the sun? We cannot cut it before the ceremony, and especially with a naked bride!"

Chapter Four: Whenever Possible, Have a Backup Plan

The strings stopped playing because they were in the full sun, the guests were sweating, and every vendor was yelling at me to start the ceremony. You can manage what you have the best you can, but when you are not surrounded by a like-minded client or a team that has your back, you have set yourself up for failure. At this point, I could not make a list of what I could have done and should have done prior to that moment. I had to make the best of what I had and get through the day and situation the best I could.

The intern ran up the driveway with a brown paper bag, shouting, "I have a tiara!" Yes! Maybe this was the turning point I needed. I ran up the stairs and handed the bride the tiara and said, "You look gorgeous; now let's put on some underwear and your dress. The guests are all waiting outside! It's time!" And she did. For some unknown reason, she just needed that tiara—I guess too many superhero movies as a child.

As the minister pronounced them husband and wife, everyone cheered as they walked down the aisle—I think more because they were happy to get out of the sun rather than because they were actually happy for the couple. As the newlyweds approached the top of the aisle, I said, "Right this way to cut the cake!"

"What? But it isn't time," said the groom.

Rule 1,089: Do not argue with the wedding planner. At this point in the day, you are happy. You do not know the full story. You do not know about the fire in the kitchen or the melted wedding cake. So just keep enjoying your day, smile, and cut the damn cake!

As the DJ played club music during the garden party, I thought to myself, *Just another hour, and this is over.* Just about then, I heard thunder. That's the special thing about Texas in May. You can check the weather all day, and a storm can pop up out of nowhere. Then came the dreaded sound that I think actually made me cry: the tornado sirens. All the guests started to run through the open-air backyard toward the house, and rain started pouring out of the sky with no warning. With one valet, I had no idea how we would get these guests to their cars. Was that even safe? At this point, I had learned all the lessons. Thank you, Lord, for reminding me again that I need a backup plan and a backbone to stand up to these client demands. But really? A tornado? Was that necessary?

As I walked into the door at home that evening, two of my high school friends had just arrived to see me. They asked me how my day was, and I thought to myself, *Where will I even begin, and they probably wouldn't even believe me! I just lived this craziness, and it is too soon to relive it again!* So, I just replied, "It was OK; why don't you tell me about your day?"

Have you ever faced anything like this when you didn't have a backup plan? Can you think of a time when preparing more would have helped you and possibly changed the results and outcome? Trust your instinct and rely on the people around you. What this situation taught me was that I needed to be interviewing my clients like they were interviewing me!

Interviewing Clients, Potential Employees, and Friends

This life is yours! It is a two-way street, every single relationship. Surrounding yourself with the right people in all aspects of life will be your backup plan! You want to be surrounded with people that will always have your back.

Clients or Customers

You do not have to take on every job. Interview them while they are interviewing you!

Ask yourself: Do this client's values align with my values? Is this project something that I want my name associated with? Even if the money is good, you only have one reputation.

Trust the inner voice in your head. If something is telling you not to do it, listen.

We are not for everybody, and everybody is not for us. That is why there are so many event planners. There may be a perfect fit for the client that is not you, and that is OK. You cannot physically be everything to everybody. This will help build your reputation and make your business in higher demand.

Even though it may not be the best fit, always be kind. Refer someone else or explain that you really may not be the best person for them. People will respect your honesty and help. They do not know what you know.

Remember, everyone you encounter is your calling card. Even though that person may not be your client, they probably have a friend that is, and they will tell them about you!

Potential Employees

This is a two-way street. You want someone that will thrive in your environment, someone that can balance your industry with family and personal life.

Ask them about their family. If they are happy in their personal life, that will translate to work. The two cannot be separate.

Friends

You do not have to be friends with everyone, but you do have to be friendly to everyone.

When you are a business owner, wife, mom, and friend, you have a lot of people in need of your time. Do you sometimes feel like saying, "Get in line"? The truth is, there are only so many hours in the day, and it is your choice. How are you going to spend them, and who are you going to spend them with?

Be intentional about friendships. If I am not intentional, time passes me by. I fill up my schedule with saying yes to everyone that asks me to do anything, and I look up at the end of the year and say, "Did I really see my *real* friends? Did I spend quality time with the people that I really want to surround myself with?"

A Sad Backup Plan

Sometimes brides can be longtime clients, and you will later plan birthdays, baby showers, or charity galas they chair, but not often do you get to plan multiple weddings for the same bride!

Another bride, I will never forget, because I planned four weddings for her that did not happen and one actual wedding that finally did happen.

We will call the bride Sheila. I met her while she was planning a birthday party for herself at her fiancé's parents' house while they were away in Aspen for the summer. She was delightful, bubbly and cheery and very creative, and she wanted all the bells and whistles for her party. I was in!

She wanted a full Marie Antoinette–themed costume party with white swans in the fountain, greeting guests as they arrived.

Unfortunately for Sheila, the engagement did not work out, but we kept in touch. A few months later, my phone rang, and it was Sheila. "Sara Fay, you are not going to believe it, but I have a new boyfriend! He is absolutely wonderful and is so kind. Just the other day, I was mentioning that I registered for the most beautiful bird china at Neiman Marcus during my first engagement and that I was sad that I never was able to get the china. Would you believe he went on my old registry, and it is still on the Neiman's website, and he bought all the bird plates just for me!" She did not even let me get a word in and continued, "So I was thinking, a bird-watching themed luncheon at his house with all my friends so they can see my new china! What do you think?" I thought to myself, *This is amazing! I love getting creative and thinking outside the box with a fun theme and not just a traditional wedding! We could really have fun with this, especially since her fiancé is paying!*

We hired gorgeous male models and dressed them in black tuxedos and rented a vintage white Rolls-Royce to hand-deliver the luncheon invitations. The men knocked on the ladies' doors with a silver tray in hand and a beautiful white box tied with a flowing green ribbon, their names written by hand in beautiful calligraphy on the box. The first recipient squealed as she opened the door. I mean, what would you think if this arrived at your door?

As she grabbed the box and ripped off the top of the box, inside lay the most gorgeous antique, gold bird-watching binoculars with a hand-tied invitation, inviting the ladies to attend the luncheon.

This is just a little background for you to fully understand the level of how much I loved dealing with these crazy clients and felt it my duty to fulfill their craziest wishes!

As their relationship progressed over the next few months, so did their wedding plans. I do not think he knew about the wedding plans, but she was definitely thinking about every possible detail. She called me and said, "Don is so busy with work, so he cannot even think about getting married. His company is having a work conference in Mexico, and I think since he will be there with his friends and colleagues already, we should just go ahead and plan the wedding during the schedule of the conference. What do you think?"

I started, "Well, I am not sure this is a very good plan. Does he know that you may surprise him with a wedding and try to get him to walk down the aisle?"

"Oh, Sara Fay," she exclaimed, "I have a backup plan! I think we should have plan A be that if he does agree to marry me that day, we can have the two flower arrangements at the altar area on the beach; could you do that diagram for me? Then we will go to the normal company cocktail hour and seated dinner that is planned—it will just now be our wedding reception! Follow me? Then, if he does not agree to marry me that day, plan B will be we just won't have the ceremony and the two arrangements that we had already paid for to be used at the ceremony can just go on the food stations at the cocktail reception. It is a perfect backup plan!" Sometimes you just must go with what the client wants; in this case, they went with plan B!

Again, this client probably was not the best client for my life balance of personal and professional life. But boy, did I love the chase! I had to learn that lesson a few times, making her crazy dreams come true, and that maybe making her wedding dreams on Thanksgiving and Christmas come true probably wasn't the best decision for my family.

Getting Caught Off Guard

When you couldn't possibly have a backup plan and cannot make it up … you just have to laugh.

Chapter Four: Whenever Possible, Have a Backup Plan

I had a bride that was worried, worried, worried! She was so worried during the planning that she got Bell's palsy, and her face became frozen. What was the saddest to me is that she was mostly worried about things that were out of her control or anyone else's control. It is hard for me to understand people like that. Why worry when we cannot control the outcome? I also have a theory that the more worried and stressed you are about details that may not matter in the big picture of things, the higher your percentages go up for rain on your wedding day!

This wedding was in the desert—a beautiful open-air tent overlooking giant boulder rocks. It was truly a one-of-a-kind scene. The ceremony had gone perfectly, and the weather was absolutely gorgeous. Everything was going as planned to schedule, and we were in what you would call the home stretch of the wedding evening. The guests had eaten, the band was playing, and not much was left on the schedule of events except the bride and groom's departure. This is always when things happen—when you least expect them. I was standing along the side of the tent enjoying the band play "This Is My House" when out of nowhere, cicadas began swarming the tent. I am not talking about a few flying bugs. There were thousands upon thousands of cicadas that came from nowhere! You could not even see your hand in front of your face, only a sea of black, and the sound of buzzing was so loud, it almost sounded like a freight train. I immediately shouted into my earpiece, "Get the cans of insect spray out of the vendor tent and spray the band first so they can keep playing!" I scurried around the dance floor, spraying the orange bottle of bug spray until it was empty. I might as well have not even sprayed. Apparently, this was a once-in-a-lifetime event that only happens once every hundred years!

Of course it happened that night. See what I mean? It wasn't rain, but it was worse! We looked at each other and laughed. Of course this is happening now of all weddings—something you completely cannot control! I am not sure exactly how long it lasted. What seemed like forever was probably ten minutes. Then suddenly, like to a conductor's cue to an orchestra, at once, all the cicadas fell to the ground and died. "What in the world?!" I exclaimed. This was one of the craziest scenes I had ever experienced. I immediately dropped the spray cans and picked up a broom and started brushing the dead black bugs from the dance floor off the side of the tent floor to the grass. I whispered to the band leader to repeat after me and say, "You wanted a once-in-a-lifetime kind of evening, and you got it! Now let's dance!"

Sometimes laughter is the only way to get through a situation when no backup plan is possible. Just laugh; it is the best medicine for everyone involved!

Chapter Four Takeaways and Reflections

Having a plan is always better than not having a plan. Go into everything you do being overprepared. It is always better to be overprepared than underprepared.

You can have plan A, plan B, and plan C, and sometimes, things still do not go as planned. Remember to remain calm. This situation, whatever it is, will pass, and later, you will look back, and it will be OK. Make sure you have the best support system around you for advice and support.

When it all falls apart, cry, laugh, and get back up. If your plan isn't working, admit it; be honest about it. Everyone is human, and there is a good chance the person on the other side of the situation will have more compassion for honesty over perfection.

Business

- What are questions you can add to your interview process to make sure you are aligned?

_____
_____
_____
_____
_____
_____

Friends

- Name five friends you would like to go on a walk with or have coffee with over the next three months. (Make sure these are people that fill up your cup!)

_____
_____
_____
_____

- Name five people that you want to have dinner with over the next three months, families or couples.

  _____
  _____
  _____
  _____
  _____

- Who are people that do not fill up your cup, who actually bring you down or give you inner anxiety, that you need to unfollow on Instagram or say *no* to the next time they reach out? This is OK to do. Be intentional!

  _____
  _____
  _____
  _____
  _____

Chapter Five

LEADING WITH FOCUS

*Leadership Roles and the Importance
of Compartmentalizing, Keeping Calm,
and Leading through Adversity*

*Laughter gives us distance. It allows us to step back
from an event, deal with it, and then move on.*

—BOB NEWHART

Leading with focus is a constant reminder to yourself to stay on track, to not get caught up in the drama of the situation, to not sit at your computer putting out fires, but to really listen to the people on your team. Hear what they are saying, follow your own instincts, and trust them. You will make mistakes, but that is the way you grow and learn as a leader.

Have you ever been in a leadership position where you did not know the best way to lead the group in front of you? When my father passed away, it was very sudden. Becoming the president of Beale Street Blues Company was literally overnight for me. I had worked for the company before but had been focused on my own events company for many years. The morning after my father died, my cell phone was constantly ringing. But one call in particular, I will never forget. It was from our corporate attorney. "Sara Fay, the bank accounts are frozen because your father's name is on the bank accounts. All the restaurants must make deposits from the sales from yesterday. We need a new president and CEO of the company to open the bank accounts and keep things running. Since you are the executor of the estate and your father left you in charge of things, this should be you. Are you willing to step in?" I did not hesitate and said, "Of course; what do I need to do?"

Right then and there, my life would change forever. I did not think. I just knew I needed to help the situation and said yes. I was a fixer at heart. I loved fixing problems. Whether it was a wedding tent collapsing or a business collapsing, I was your girl.

When I look back at that day, I think the "not thinking and doing" is what made it happen. If I had sat there analyzing all the problems, things that I did not understand or know about the business, then I would have completely scared myself and talked myself out of it.

Do you ever do that? Do you ever think, "Am I good enough for this position? Do I have the skillset for this position? What if they figure out that I really do not know what I am doing?" Does anyone really know what they are doing? No, they take all the experiences they have from their particular through line of their own life, weave them together, and voilà! You have a unique skillset that no one else in the world has. Think about that. No one else in the entire world has your skillset, your exact experiences in the exact way that they happened to you. Your own personal through line is like your fingerprint. Now it is your job to take that and make your own fingerprint on your family, friends, community, and the world.

What do you do? "I am a wedding planner ... oh, actually ... I run a restaurant group!"

It still sounds funny to say! This was never my dream, running restaurants. It was my father's dream—or was it? He started as an accountant, and life led him to this. I do not think he sat down and outlined the exact plan of where his life was going to take him, but here we are. Here we all are. It's exciting, energizing, and beautifully messy.

OK, now I was in charge, but how was I going to lead a seasoned team? Some of them had been with the company for over twenty years. They knew the ins and outs, all the stories, all the history—they knew Restaurant 101. I remembered some of the stories my father had told me over the years, but I sure did not know how to run a restaurant. However, I had owned and run two prior businesses, also both in hospitality. They had the same elements of those businesses, with sales, managing people, managing clients, and creating atmospheres through food, beverage, design, and music. I could do this. I just had to find the right way to lead.

The Boss's Daughter

Earning respect in this role required a delicate balance of listening, setting boundaries, and asserting control. This is a slippery slope, and earning respect takes time. This is a hard position to be in because you have a target on your head before you even arrive that says you have been handed this position and did not earn it. You are starting with less respect than even an unqualified person walking in off the street. People are probably taking bets on how long you will last. I know everyone thought I would fail or sell the company. I just took that as more fuel to prove them wrong. I have never liked people telling me I can't do something. To that, I say, "*Watch me!*"

Gaining respect from a new team is not something that is earned overnight. My team and employees had been with the company for years and needed time to watch me, to see what I would do and to see how I would lead. I knew this, and I knew all eyes were on me. I needed a road map. I could not call my dad and see what his plans were, and I did not necessarily want or need to follow his plan. I did not even know if this was something that I really wanted to do. So, I had to focus on what I did know. I needed to do things my way, but in the right way, and I needed time to lead effectively. Here are some of the actions that I have found can help when you are leading in a situation, whether it's your business, team, family, or committee. Leadership is leadership.

How to Build a Road Map to Lead Effectively

Listen and Find the Most Trusted Inner Circle to Help You

You cannot do this alone. You cannot come into a leadership position and think you know it all and make changes, because you don't know it all and can't possibly know it all. I first had many one-on-one meetings with the four people that I considered the closest corporate leaders who worked with my father. There were *many* people wanting my attention, calling, texting, emailing. All had different stories, and I did not know who to trust. I could not ask my father what the real story was, so I had to make these decisions on my own.

- Who is your inner trusted circle?

  _____

  _____

  _____

- How can you incorporate these people more into your daily life and routine?

  _____

  _____

  _____

Put Up Boundaries and Walls

I created a chain of command with the inner leadership group. I realized quickly that so many people had taken advantage of my father through getting to him and pulling at his heartstrings. While this can be nice in some ways, I had to be in charge, lead, and know who I could trust before I broke down these walls. This is one of the best things that I did. Remember, putting up walls is OK when they are boundaries!

- What boundaries do you need to set in your life, and with who?

  _____

  _____

  _____

- What steps can you immediately take to set those boundaries?

  _____

  _____

  _____

Silence the Noise

There will be a lot of noise around you—gossip, rumors, talking … silence this and these people. When someone starts talking and you know that the story is not leading in a positive direction, then shut them down. This will immediately let them know that you are in charge, and you are not interested in the middle-school narrative. You do not have time for it, and your team will be better for it.

- What noise in your life do you need to silence?

  _____

  _____

  _____

Manage Your Time

Schedule each hour of your day, and make sure each call or meeting you are having is productive. Ask yourself, can this task be done by someone else on my team? If yes, then *delegate it*! If no, it stays on your calendar.

Also ask yourself, is this meeting important for the growth or sales of my company, or is this something I just felt like I had to say yes to? If you feel like you had to say yes—and believe me, I have learned this the hard way—then maybe you should say no. We only have a certain number of hours in the day, and you cannot do it all, not to mention also adding time into your schedule for when you will turn off work and be present with your family or friends. This is really the only way I have made both family life and business life work—by turning off work when I am with my family. For years, I would always be on my laptop at night because I had so much work that had to be done. I could see it in the eyes of my husband and kids the second I would open my laptop: the look of someone who just lost their puppy. I hated that look. After seeing it time after time, I knew they needed my attention, and I needed to be more present and get my work done during the day so I could be present for my family in the evening.

- What three things can you do to help you manage your time better?

    _____

    _____

    _____

Compartmentalize

Compartmentalizing is really the only way I have gotten through the last few years, with all aspects of my life: work, friendship, family. You need a box for everything and everyone. You cannot get overwhelmed by thinking about everything on your plate all at once. You will go crazy, probably cry, and be completely paralyzed. Or at least, I would have been. For me, it was impossible to maintain focus or be in the moment unless I did this.

To start, put things in different boxes in your mind. Write it *all* down, whether this is a to-do list, your thoughts, journaling. If you write it down, you can always go back to it later, but it releases the anxious thought from your head. Start simple with two boxes: "Work or To-Dos" and "Family/Friends." Try not to let the boxes overlap.

In the beginning of my career and for many years, this idea did not exist. My work was my family, and my family was my work. My closest friends were people I worked with. We spent holidays together. They knew everything about my life—until I quit working there. Then it all went away. It felt like a divorce. Even though those memories and deep friendships will always be there deep down, things changed. It was not the healthiest situation for me, my marriage, or my work. Now I try my hardest to have these two defined boxes. This does not mean you cannot be a true friend to people you work with. You always need to listen, be kind, and be there for support. But keep the boxes separate. Trust me! Try it.

- What is on your plate that is overwhelming you that you can compartmentalize into these boxes right now?

_____

_____

_____

Dive In

No matter what your business is, you will gain the most respect from your team by them actually seeing you work. Roll up your sleeves and do all the jobs. In my first event-planning job, there were the cute girls in the sales office in heels and skirts, and there was the production team. This is very similar to restaurants. You have the front of house with the managers, hosts, and servers, and you have the back of house with the kitchen staff of chefs, cooks, the prep team, and dishwashers. They have to work together to have a successful business, and this all begins with respect.

    I truly felt like the production team always respected me, and I think it was because I dove in and did their jobs on any given day. I drove the delivery trucks when needed, I loaded the trucks alongside them with supplies and flowers, and I would grab a broom and sweep the floors. Did I do this every day? No. Is it in the best interest of the company for me to do this every day? No; I needed to be in the sales office bringing in the sales so that the production team had a job. *But* there is a fine balance here of understanding what all levels of your team go through on a daily basis, and working alongside them is a great way to gain their respect. I believe this is true for all levels of leadership. You may be in a leadership position for a nonprofit or charity or on the PTA or a committee at school. Any good leader has the respect of the team, and that is the best way to lead the team forward. With their respect, you can get them to do anything for you.

> - What is something you have been wanting to dive into but have been too nervous to try?
>
> _____
>
> _____
>
> _____

Build Trust

Trust takes time. It probably took me two full years to gain the trust of my new corporate team. This sounds like a long time, and as I said earlier, it is not something that happens overnight. I found that it was necessary to lay out a road map for them, showing things that I knew needed to happen in a certain order before other things could happen. While many of the details changed, I stuck to this overarching road map and followed through with the things that I said I was going to do. I feel like making a promise or setting a plan helps your team to have hope and faith in you, and then following through with those promises builds trust.

- What is your road map to fulfilling a promise?

_____

_____

_____

Take Control

I have always liked being in control and being the leader in charge. While you can improve your leadership skills in so many ways, many people are just born this way.

I think that is why I have never liked snow skiing. The feeling of flying through the air and not being in control of my own body? Not for me. Now don't get me wrong, I do love tequila, but at least my feet are on the ground!

With your team, it is different. You do not want to come across as bossy or rude. You also do not want to make decisions too quickly without assessing the situation fully. I have also learned that the hard way, especially after being thrown overnight into a business I knew nothing about. I could not come in and take charge with a strong arm when I technically did not know what I was doing. I had to learn. I had to listen to those around me. I had to be a sponge and soak up everything in the environment. Now, this did not mean that I had to agree with everyone or everything in the environment. At the beginning, it was very hard for me to hold my tongue on certain issues regarding the restaurant. I had come from very high-end design and events, and now I was walking into restaurants that were also blues clubs. While they were very different, I knew what standards needed to be brought in. I will never forget the first Christmas that I walked into B. B. King's in Memphis after taking over the company. The team was so happy that I had arrived. They had the biggest smiles and were so excited to show me that they decorated for Christmas. They took so much pride in what they had done. I took a deep breath and smiled. I could not take that smile off their faces, and I was new here. From the looks of it, they had bought whatever hodgepodge Christmas decorations that did not sell the day after Christmas last year on sale. I told myself to smile and tell them thank you and that they did a great job.

It was really sweet how much they cared and how much they wanted to make me happy. I did not tear them down and tell them it was ugly. But I did go to the Dallas Market Center in July to buy Christmas decorations!

They had no idea that for the last twenty years, people had hired my company to decorate people's houses for Christmas. It was my thing. I loved it! I *live* for Christmas decorations. But I had to remember I was walking into something new, and it was all about timing, respect, and trust. They did not know me, and I did not really know them. We needed to "date" a little longer. Two years later, and we have completely renovated the restaurant. We redid the floors, painted the walls, and brought it up to the decor standards that I am proud of. But we did it together. We took everything off the walls. I went to the storage units and personally hung the memorabilia from my father's personal collection on the walls. It felt good to be in there working alongside our employees. Them seeing me diving in and actually physically taking control of every inch of the restaurant went a long way. I could see it in their eyes. I now had their respect and trust. I now have established the rule that no one buys anything for the restaurant or puts anything on the walls without getting it approved by me. If I had done that on day one, I would have sounded like a tyrant.

They would have hated me, and many would have probably quit. It was all about the timing, the rollout, and the way taking control was approached that made it work.

> - What are three things you can do immediately to take control of your home, project, or work?
>
> _____
>
> _____
>
> _____

Taking Control in the Bahamas

This was just too funny not to share. Planning weddings on islands lives up to the saying "on island time." We had planned every single inch of the wedding, and the installation timeline was down to the minute. I felt so confident going into the week of the installation. We had so many site visits and worked very closely with the local tent company, who were incredibly professional operators for an island. We had perfectly staked where the tent was going, so I was not worried. For our typical wedding installs, the tent would take two weeks to put up before the wedding. To help with costs, the tent company put the tent and floor up the week before I arrived, and I would be there for the second week when all the decor was being installed in the tent.

I arrived on Monday, July 10, the week before the wedding, and walked up to the tent at about 2:00 p.m. The waves were crashing onto the beach, and the sun peeked out from behind the smallest cloud, casting a beautiful shadow of palm leaves on the tent. For a moment, I caught myself dreaming of how gorgeous Saturday would be in this picture-perfect quiet setting. Then I snapped back to reality and thought to myself, "Wait a minute, this is a little too quiet! Where are all the vendors? Why is no one working?" I pulled out the thick three-ring binder from my bag and turned to the timeline tab. According to my schedule, there were supposed to be five vendors here! I immediately pulled out my phone and called the tent company. I got the answering machine. I called the salesperson's cell phone, and she answered. It was loud in the background, as I could hear the sounds of Junkanoo and what sounded like a parade. "Aroxie, where are the guys? I was expecting them to be working at the tent, and it looks like we are a few days behind schedule."

"Oh yeah, it is the Bahamian Independence Day, so everyone is off work celebrating for three days," she said with not a care in the world.

"What? You never told me this! But we cannot lose the next three days of the schedule. Why did you not tell me my schedule wouldn't work, or about this holiday?" I said curtly. "Don't worry, it will all get done!"

It will get done! You tell that to the mother of the bride that has been planning this in her dreams for the past twenty-five years ever since her daughter was born! That's the thing about islands. Somehow it always works out, but I wondered how they ever did a wedding when I wasn't there! No worries in the world; grab a rum punch and it will be OK! I knew I could make this happen, but it would be tight. My biggest concern was the mother of the bride. What was I going to do about her? She would lose her mind if she saw the schedule wasn't being followed. I had to take control of this situation. There was no other choice. I had to lock her out—literally. I instructed my team to zip-tie all the tent doors closed so she could not come in the tent to see how far behind we were. I adjusted the schedule and knew we would make it work. I would be there to delegate to the local teams when they arrived back to work to get us back on American time. As long as I could keep her out of the tent, it would be OK! Would you believe it worked?

My phone rang that night. It was the mother. "Sara Fay, I am at the tent, and it is all dark, so I cannot see in, and the doors are all locked. I really wanted to see the progress."

"Really?" I said. "Oh yes, the tent company did tell me they were going to lock the tent. It's a security issue. We just want to make sure everything is secure and safe!" I heard her reply, "Wow, you think of everything!"

Staying Calm

In all of these situations, I feel like being known for being calm is what set me apart from other wedding planners. Remember, if you are calm, everyone else is calm. They are all looking at you. No matter what is happening around you, stay calm in front of your team. If you need a minute, take a minute. Remove yourself from the situation. It is funny the similarities in raising kids and running a business, especially approaching the teenage years. I have learned to put myself in time-out this year, and it is one of the best tools I have learned. I look back at the times I lost my temper in front of my employees or with my family, and I regret every single time. It is not a good look. If you feel yourself getting overwhelmed and your heart racing, step away. Put yourself in time-out. Try it. I promise you will thank me.

After you step away, try these few things:

- Breathe.
- Drink a glass of water.
- Write down your frustrations.
- Write down what you can control and what you cannot.

- Is now the time to approach the situation, or do you need to circle back another time when things are less heated?

  _____
  _____

- If now is the time to reenter, write down what you are going to say.

  _____
  _____

- Are you the one that needs to apologize?

  _____
  _____

- What helps you to stay calm in stressful moments?

  _____
  _____
  _____
  _____

Chapter Five Takeaways and Reflections

Look at life and work from the perspective of others. You helping their livelihood translates into them helping your livelihood.

Do not forget to be grateful. Thank the people who have gotten you to where you are today. Seriously, stop reading and send a text to three people. You know who they are! Maybe you have not spoken to them in years, but appreciation matters, and a simple text will mean all the world to them. Even the most prestigious mentors have a bad day and may need your text right this second.

Make a note to make a note! Say thank you. A handwritten thank you goes so far. People do not do it enough anymore, so when you do get a handwritten note in the mail, that impression of that person is stamped into your mind forever. They go in a different category in your brain: the "raised right" category!

If you have good leadership skills, you can lead any team. Think about it. Why do you follow a leader? I follow people that I believe are truthful and honest, are fun to be around, are energizing, and make me feel better after being with them. I follow people that I want to be like. It doesn't matter what you are selling or doing; if you are passionate and believe in what you are selling or doing, then you can lead.

Chapter Six

BALANCING PERSONAL AND PROFESSIONAL LIFE

Balancing Personal and Professional Lives to Achieve Harmony and Find Fulfillment

You are the average of the five people you spend the most time with.

—JIM ROHN

Balancing personal and professional life is less about achieving a perfect equilibrium and much more about being present and setting boundaries that protect your well-being.

I think we all make the mistake of assuming our friends and colleagues will innately have the same morals and values as we do. I have learned the hard way this is very wrong to assume. There are so many good people out there, but most people put themselves first. Reflecting on this thought, I think personally, I have trusted people a little too much, especially in business. I have learned that you can pretend like you are all one big, happy family and create that type of work environment, but in the end, it is business. It is much better to draw the lines between friendship and colleagues up-front. That does not mean that you cannot be a friend and give friendly advice, but it does mean that you need to be careful to not assume they would act as you would. I have had business partners and close colleagues who, with the flip of a switch, turned on me. This is a hard lesson to learn, but somewhere along the way, it was my fault. I was naive. You need to protect yourself in all relationships. But this does not mean you cannot be your authentic self. In talking to attorneys, they always want you to dot every I and cross every T. Just like in a prenuptial agreement, you never think it is going to happen to you. When you sign the prenup before you get married, you are in love and have all the warm and fuzzies. This is the same in any relationship. Being up-front about expectations and what they should be can only help you in the long run. I think looking back on all the business mistakes that I have made, this was my hardest lesson: trusting too much.

That does not mean I now look at new opportunities with new people and do not see hope. I try to learn from the mistakes that I made and move forward, add it to the list of the downward curve in my through line, one that I can use to make the curve go back up! I do have a little bit more of a guard that goes up each time with new opportunities and new relationships now. Naturally, I try to find the good in people and go from there.

Can you relate to these stories? Find your people. Find the people that share your morals, values, and goals, and trust them. Lean on them. If they are happy for you and you know they are cheering you on, trust them. If they are jealous of your success or happiness, move on.

And remember, life is not all about work. Have fun as much as you possibly can!

Work Hard, Play Hard

I have always worked hard. I have always had an internal drive to do more. But there is a fine balance. For years, I was working so hard, I was missing out on life—missing friends' weddings, missing family times, missing connecting with friends for the sake of work. It all looked so good on paper and so glamorous when my weddings would be printed in the magazines. But at what personal cost? I would be back home after a wedding on Sunday and so focused on the number of likes from random people that I didn't even know on my Instagram. That's when I knew I needed to draw that line, put it all down, and focus on my family.

Some of this is good. I think when you are young, it is important to work hard and do all the jobs. Learn all the things that you can. But there is a fine balance to know when to turn it off so you can reset. I have found that giving up on times with your friends and family just to work hard leaves your cup empty. Sometimes you have to learn this for yourself if you have a hard project, deadline, or, in my case, a large wedding.

What is it all for? You cross the finish line, then it's over. That one day of feeling fulfilled is over, and you are on to the next thing, starting at empty, feeling empty. The connections stop with other people if you ignore them or are so focused on work that you lose touch. Relationships take work and time.

But you also need to play hard, whether with your kids or with your friends! Go to the concert, eat the French fries, dance on the tables, drink the champagne, sing out loud, and live *your* best life as much as you possibly can. We are not guaranteed tomorrow. So, play when you can, whatever that means to you!

There were many times where I felt like if I was succeeding at work, I was failing at family life, and if things were great at home, then I was neglecting work. Do you ever feel that way?

Is there such thing as balance? I really do not think so. I think it is more about presence. Learning to truly be present where you are and in that moment is the single thing that has helped me the most.

Do *not* feel bad you are not at home when you are at work. Give that minute your absolute full attention, and if you can't, then that is when you need the day off. You need the time to focus on what is taking up the space in your head, what is sitting there rent-free but consuming all your thoughts.

Take a minute and journal. What is taking up space in your head right now and not allowing you to focus on what you need to focus on? What daily changes can you make to help you separate these to-dos in your head? Do you compartmentalize?

For me, it is waking up earlier than the rest of my household. On the days I do this, I feel like I can do anything that day. Just making my daily to-do list and getting those items out of my head allows me to be present later and not feel like I am starting the day behind.

This usually leads to overwhelming guilt, a feeling that many working parents know and experience.

The Mom Guilt Is Real!

I spent way too much time feeling guilty, racing to carpool pickup just to hear my daughter say, "Mom, why aren't you in workout clothes like all the other moms? Why can't you be like them?" I carried so much guilt around the first few years of motherhood.

If I was at a play group, I was having anxiety that I needed to be at work. When I was at work, I had anxiety that the nanny was at play group and the other moms were judging me, or that my daughter would be scarred for life because her mother wasn't cutting her carrots perfectly and was more focused on a meeting.

I really struggled. I wanted to work, because I loved it and it filled my cup up more than sitting at play group, but I was not doing either well, and something had to change.

Are you struggling to find balance between two sides of your life tugging at you? Which areas of your life feel out of balance? Who is putting this pressure on you? What small changes can you make to help address it?

For me, I was putting pressure on myself. No one else was putting this pressure on me.

Why do I have this inner fight in my head? Do you ever feel that way? What steps can you take today to stop the inner dialogue of guilt?

Who in your life is putting pressure on you or you feel judges you? Maybe this person does not need to be someone you have around you.

PRO TIP

If there are people around you that give you anxiety or make you feel like you are having to prove yourself or be someone you are not (like a mean girl), then listen to that inner voice and walk away. Friends should be like a faucet, constantly filling your cup up until you say, "My cup is full, I am happy, and I have been built up, not torn down, by the people I surround myself with."

At any age, that kind of friend feels good! In middle school, you want to be sitting at that table, invited to that party, wanted as part of a group. Think about it: when someone

> *calls and you see their name on your phone, do you instantly feel anxiety but still call them a friend?*
>
> *No matter your age, that feeling doesn't change as you get older. The only difference is you begin to recognize that feeling inside of you and that you have a choice, and you are in control of your own life, the choices you make, and who your friends and sometimes work colleagues are.*
>
> *Don't expect everyone to be like you or to take the high road. Only you can decide to take the high road.*

When I Finally Got It

For me, it took getting pregnant to learn to choose myself and my body over my career. This was a hard lesson to learn.

During my first pregnancy, I had a miscarriage while I was executing an event during the holidays. I was cuing the Dallas Cowboys Cheerleaders to run out to make an appearance. In the middle of their performance, I ran to the bathroom. My biggest fear at the time had come true. I saw blood. What did this mean? But I could not leave the party! We had been working on this event for months, and now it was showtime. I could not leave! But in this moment, I needed to choose my health and my pregnancy over my job. I really had never done this before. Before this day, my events and my career had come first. If I was sick before, I would get a steroid shot and an IV—anything to stay there and make sure every detail of the event was perfect. This time, it was different. It was real. I had another life to look after that was not my own. I had a family and had to change the way I thought about a lot of things.

I gathered some other girls on my planning team and made sure the party was in good hands, and I snuck out the back door. My husband picked me up, and we raced to the emergency room. I did have a miscarriage, but there was still one heartbeat. It turned out there were twins, and the one heartbeat turned into my beautiful Grace. All in God's perfect timing, but at that moment, I realized, how was I going to keep up this pace? I will never know for sure, but did my hours, stress, and hard work contribute to my miscarriage? But I loved my job! It was not a job; it was my career, my identity. It was who I was. That is how people knew me. That is how I was valued as a person, or I thought at the time that was my only value.

I struggled with the inner dialogue, a true inner fight with myself of what I would do. I worked for the best of the best. How could I, in my mind, halfway do this? This was an all-or-nothing career. You had to always be available, or so I thought. I did not realize it yet, but I was going through what would be one of the biggest learning experiences of my life.

How do you do it all?

You don't.

At least, not all at once.

You do it in steps, in increments, in compartments.

And that is the only way you can enjoy every step of the way!

The Struggle Is Real

Now, this lesson wasn't taught in a day. I had to keep being reminded and reminded and reminded of this.

As I got closer to my due date, I was also in full swing of wedding season. We had a large wedding that I had spent a year working on and had countless meetings with the clients who I had come to know well. That is the thing. You know how much they care, which also makes you care so much. It becomes personal, not just work. It is creating something special and bringing their dreams to life for the most important day of their life.

This particular wedding was at the clients' home, overlooking a beautiful lake, one of the most gorgeous settings for a wedding with the ceremony tucked in a grove of oak trees and the reception under a white tent on the tennis courts—well, a perfect setting on the perfect weather day. I had diligently checked the weather, and there was no weather activity on the radar. But as I've said before, Texas tornadoes come out of nowhere!

A line of valet attendants greeted guests clad in their summer tuxedos as they stepped out of the long row of waiting cars. About fifty guests had been seated of the two hundred expected guests as it started to sprinkle. What? But there was nothing on the radar! I ran over to the security tent, and the security officer pulled up the radar. Lightning was spotted a mile away, and a tornado had touched down two miles away. The sirens started to blare. What was I going to do? It was OK; we had a wonderful ceremony rain plan inside the clients' sixteen-car garage. *Shoot*—we did not set up the rain plan because it was not going to rain. As long as the bride was calm, we could handle this. We hurried the guests underneath the covered walkway as soaked valet attendants, servers, and I carried chairs inside the massive garage. Somehow, we were able to move all two hundred guests into the covered area in a few minutes. I had to break it to the bride that we had to move the ceremony inside. As the guests left the garage and walked outside, it stopped raining, and a huge rainbow appeared. I thought, *wow*! I was in the clear. Thank the Lord all was well and there was no more rain for the rest of the evening, because we really did not have a good rain plan for the reception.

Another lesson I have learned is don't high-five yourself or pat yourself on the back for a job well done until it is completely finished—like, the next day finished! Finally, toward the end of the evening, I sat on the curb for the first time that day. I remember just sitting on the curb crying as cramps tightened in my stomach. What was this all for? What was this worth? But I loved it! How could I take care of myself, my family, and my unborn child and actually do what I love? Was it possible? I did not want to pick. I wanted it all.

About thirty minutes later after the last guest had left and the lights were turned off, I got into my car to drive home. I did not feel right. My cramps were getting closer and closer. Were these contractions? I could not drive any longer. I pulled over into the grocery store parking lot and called Merrick once again to pick me up. I heard the inner dialogue in my head: *Right, I could not drive all the way home, but the wedding was great! Sara Fay, stop putting clients and weddings before your own health! Something has to change.*

The Final Straw

Eleven years later ... yes, eleven years. This was one reason why I wrote this book. Learn from me; don't wait eleven years! After constantly reinventing ways to balance work, do what I love, plan weddings, be a mom, be a wife, and be a friend, I realized I needed to tie all of these experiences together.

How could I bring everything together? What is my purpose? Why am I Grace and Walker's mom and not someone else's mom? Why am I Merrick's wife? How do I take all these experiences, everything I have learned along the way, and make something useful out of them—the good, the bad, the sad, the ups, and the downs—and tie them together for good?

At this point in time, Grace was better. She was back in school. I had weddings that I had committed to years in advance, so it was a slow process to having weddings off my plate. My life was still not my own. I would schedule a meeting and then get a call from school to pick her up. I needed to be available. I needed to be present. I wanted to be present. Nothing else mattered when I got that call except to get to her.

One thing Merrick and I both felt strongly about is that we did not want anyone to ever experience what we went through with our child. It is an ugly disease, so ugly, most people don't talk about it. We decided to be vulnerable. We decided to tell our story. I knew some people might not understand our why for doing this, but if our story could help someone else to get an early diagnosis and ultimately help them avoid our experience, then it was worth it.

We started the Grace Fund to raise money for autoimmune research. Being on the patient advocate side, you see firsthand how much is still unknown in medicine and how much research is needed. Personally and selfishly, it made us feel like at least we could piece together some good from a terrible situation, and that made us feel better. It did. I had some knowledge that could help others.

At the beginning when Grace was sick, all I wanted to do was talk to someone that had been in my shoes. It was hard to go to the school pickup and hear other moms talking about their Botox appointment that day when I was so sad. This really goes for anything you are going through. You just never know what people are going through, but their eyes will tell you. Be there for them and be a friend. All I could do was listen. I could talk to other moms experiencing similar situations and give them advice. I did not have a solution, a cure, but I did have time. I could talk to them and listen and offer any advice that I had learned through my journey. The feeling I got in connecting with these parents was better than any feeling I ever got from planning a wedding. This was what life is all about: connecting with others. Be the through line in your neighbor's life. Be the connector.

What knowledge do you have that is special that you could share with others? I promise this will help you even more than it will help them!

Chapter Six Takeaways and Reflections

You never think it will happen to you. While writing this book, I felt a lump on my pelvic area. I assumed it was just a bump and would go away. I did not think much of it and went about my daily life. A few months later, I decided I should go to the doctor just to be safe. He said it was probably a lymph node and would most likely dissipate and to watch it and come back in a month. A month quickly went by as my schedule was overly jam-packed with work, kids, sports, friends, and life. I squeezed the appointment in between calls. As I walked into the sterile room and sat on the table with a white paper sheet, I thought to myself, *What if this is something?*

Dr. Hunt walked in and asked me if it was any better or the same. I said that it had gotten a little larger and more defined. He urged me to go right away and get a sonogram. After the sonogram, I got in the car as tears rolled down my face. A sadness had overcome me. I thought to myself, *When you have a scare like this, how does your day change? Who do you call? What do you clear from your calendar? What is important and not important in that moment? What did I learn from Grace's illness and COVID quiet times?*

the THROUGH *line*

I feel like we all learned lessons about life and slowing down during the first few weeks of the pandemic. We learned about what is important and not important, about what is filler on our schedules and what can be cut out. But why am I back to acting like I did pre-2020? Why am I filling up every minute? How would I change the way that I live life if the doctor calls this afternoon and says it is cancer in my lymph node? Why does it take a life-threatening scare like this to make me wake up and change? Thankfully, everything was clear on my scan, but it made me really think.

If you were told today that you had cancer, what would you do? How would you spend your time? Who would you call? What would you eat?

I challenge you to make a list. I love lists. I love crossing off lists. I love the feeling of accomplishment. If you were told you have cancer, what would you do?

Here is my list:

- I would light a candle.
- I would pray.
- I would want to be with my husband, my kids, my mom, and my sister. I would want to be with them all the time, as much as possible. I would say no to monotonous things taking my time away from them.
- I would figure out how to work smarter not harder and spend more time with family and friends who care about me like family instead of working so hard on a project that is thankless.
- I would listen. I would listen to my family and friends and their needs and try my hardest to be there for them.
- I would go outside more. I would go on a walk. I would sit on the porch and listen to music.

- Really, the above list is all I need to make me happy. What does your list look like?

  _____
  _____
  _____
  _____
  _____

- Are there new opportunities in your life that you are afraid of? What are they?

  _____
  _____
  _____
  _____
  _____

- What leap of faith should you take in your own life? Do you have a burning inner voice telling you to take the leap? What is it?

  _____
  _____
  _____
  _____
  _____

- Have you trusted people too much in relationships? How would you go into that relationship now if you could do it again? Would you set boundaries?

  _____

  _____

  _____

  _____

  _____

- Have you not put enough trust in people?

  _____

  _____

  _____

  _____

  _____

Chapter Seven

PRESERVING OUR FAMILIES, CULTURE, HISTORY, AND BUSINESSES

The beautiful thing about learning is that nobody can take it away from you.

—B. B. KING

Preservation is about honoring our past while creating a legacy for the future, whether in our homes, businesses, or families. How do we preserve buildings, homes, restaurants, and the stories of the people behind them? I want my kids to know that history. Merrick is from New Orleans, and the rich history from both our cities is unparalleled. While parts of both are dirty and run down, so are parts of every city. I do feel that it is our job to teach our kids and others about this history so it lives on. I am self-diagnosed (and my friends would agree) as crazy!

Houses started being torn down around our house in Dallas, and every street started to become this uniformity of white boxes with no charm. I saw this happening on all levels: homes, businesses, even what our kids were wearing to school. It was all the same. I saw our city losing the individuality and uniqueness that made it so special. One day, I was scrolling through Instagram, and I saw a house come across my feed. We were not looking to move, but something about this house made me stop and keep looking. It was one hundred years old and needed a lot of love. But for some reason, I looked past the dated curtains, out-of-date bathrooms, and 1980s kitchen, and all I saw were fireplaces, arches, and moldings.

I did not need another project, to say the least. My plate was full and overflowing, but something in this house called to me. Merrick and I went to see it. As we walked in, he immediately told the realtor we were just there to look and were not moving. She immediately said, "Oh, you can tear the whole house down; it is a great lot!" But my eyes were twinkling as I turned the first corner. Even in its current state, which had not been touched in decades, the idea of bringing this house back to life excited me. I gazed at the fireplace and tried to imagine what dinner parties had happened in this room in the 1920s, what business deals, life experiences, and life decisions had been made right in this room! I could feel the energy, see the pearls and the silver trays, and hear the music. I felt somewhat challenged by the "You can tear it down" statement to bring the house back to life! And so we did.

Living in Dallas, where there is a shiny new build on every corner, I am sure many people look at us as if we were completely crazy to take on this project. But I feel like we are stewarding something, building a home that can be passed down to our children and their children. It is not just a house but a home, and I knew this home would bring my family happiness.

Life is messy. If the margins in your day are filled with things that are giving you and your family life, then do it! Just go for it! And every time I walk into this house, even looking at pipes and studs, my soul is filled with joy, and that is what it is all about!

Chapter Seven: Preserving Our Families, Culture, History, and Businesses

Passing It Down

I think it is important for our communities and our children to have a through line to our past. That is what makes us all so unique and special. I love the idea of creating this through line for our new old home, a house that could have been torn down and the line ended before us. The stories and history could have ended with us. Now it will go on to tell another story and hopefully many more stories for another one hundred years. Hopefully the home will have many parties, gatherings, meals, slumber parties, and football games. The thought of all the memories that were made in the house over the past hundred years and the memories our family can make, and then thinking of the future to come over the next one hundred years, leaves me excited and energized.

One day, the construction team cut through an opening in the front entry hall to find a small, green, slightly stained book with gold font, titled *The King of the Golden River*. The publication date on the book was 1926, and in cursive handwriting on the inside left cover page was written the name Lenora Banton, with the address of the house below it. We researched the name, and it turns out the little girl was the granddaughter of the original owners of the property. The entry porch was enclosed around 1926, and she must have been reading on the porch and left her book there and it accidentally got enclosed in the wall. How incredible this artifact was, left in the wall for ninety-eight years. How unbelievable to think about what life was like at the house back then. It was a farm with horses and chickens. Life was much simpler then. Lovers Lane was a dirt road, and what is now very much in the middle of the city was out in the country.

I truly believe that it is important to know where you came from, really understand and appreciate where you came from, whether good or bad, in order to know where you are going. With your personal life and business life, appreciating the past and what has happened before you can only help you to learn from the mistakes, maybe circle back to a lost art, and help you get back to the basics of what is important, like sitting on the front porch reading a book just like Lenora did.

What Makes You Special?

Recently with our restaurants, I have been trying to think about what we have that makes us unique from other restaurant groups. Seriously, think about what you have in your business or your life that makes you or your business unique.

In a sea of dining establishments, our family's restaurants stand out with a distinct melody—a tune that sings the blues of B. B. King and whispers the stories of legends past. It's not just about the food or the ambiance; it's about the narrative we weave into every experience, making our patrons not just customers but custodians of a rich, musical heritage.

When my father passed away, we had nine restaurants and seven different brands. I began thinking about this a lot. The restaurant business is a very cutthroat business. You must always be on your toes and always be delivering top quality and service. Sometimes you only have one shot with a guest, and if that experience is not great, then they will not be back. It is hard to make it in the industry, and it requires a lot of trial and error and hard work. Our concepts currently include B. B. King's Blues Club, both in Memphis, Tennessee, and Montgomery, Alabama, Itta Bena Fine Dining in both Memphis and Montgomery, and Lucille's Eatery in Montgomery.

The four concepts that we had previously were great concepts, but there was no through line to tie them together. I am all about a through line. Whether it is tying in all the details with an event, a

Chapter Seven: Preserving Our Families, Culture, History, and Businesses

wedding, a restaurant, a brand, retail, etc., you must have a through line that tells the story.

What is your story? What are you selling, and what about your business makes you different?

In our case, B. B. King is what made us different. I like to say anyone can open a restaurant, especially with American-style cuisine. I had to really take a hard look at what was our through line and what tied us all together. Our remaining three concepts all tie back to B. B. King.

B. B. King was born in a small town in Mississippi called Itta Bena. This makes it the perfect name for our speakeasy-style fine dining concept in its original location on Beale Street above B. B. King's Blues Club. You walk up the fire escape to white tablecloth booths tucked in between perfectly patinaed wood-shuttered panels and the blue-tinted window glow of the neon lights of Beale Street below. The black-and-white images on the walls of Elvis, B. B. King, Booker T. and the MG's, Isaac Hayes, and many more tell the stories of all the musicians that have graced these walls before. These are the stories that I want my kids to know.

Today, so many restaurants are bright and shiny. They have the hot new plate, new fusion of styles, and new decor. But what we have is special. I wanted to take this and play off of it. There are not many places where you have so much history, so much culture oozing out around you. You can feel the soul through the music, the atmosphere, and the food. I love it here.

Every successful event and every thriving restaurant is at its core about the people. Whether it's understanding the nuances of a bridal party's dynamics or catering to a diner's palate, the ability to connect on a personal level is what transforms a business into a community.

It's a cascade of interactions where each individual, each story, adds to the richness of the collective experience.

Are you creating something that can also be preserved? A close friend said to me, "Leaving something to our children, whether it is passing down our moral code, a home, land, or a family business, is the greatest thing we can share with our children." What do you have that you can preserve? This could be through your work, your children, charity, or a leadership position. There are many ways in your life that you can preserve things for the future.

It certainly does not have to be an old home. It could be a business and setting up systems that will stand in place much longer than just the period of time that you are in charge to set future generations up for success.

Think about it. What can you do to make a difference? What can you leave as your legacy to the generations to come after you?

What Made Our Family Special?

We had been through something very unique with Grace's illness. It was something we did not want to shout from the rooftops for our family's privacy, but it was also something that we did not want anyone else to ever have to experience. We had the knowledge of a unique experience and had information to share. We had learned a lot. We knew we had knowledge and resources that could help others.

Back when Grace was hospitalized and we felt like we had nowhere to turn, we found Dr. Greenberg. We actually did not meet him in person the first time. A robot came down the hallway, opened the door, and wheeled on in. Dr. Greenberg's face was on the screen. Merrick and I were immediately surprised at how personable talking to a robot felt. The machine would tilt its screen to the left and address his arm toward me when speaking. We didn't care. All we cared about was that he had seen this illness before. Grace has what is called seronegative autoimmune encephalitis. What that means is that we do not know what antibodies in her brain are being attacked. Dr. Greenberg has an eloquent way of speaking so we can understand what this means. He says, "Think of the galaxy. We have names for about a hundred stars, but there are hundreds of thousands of stars in the galaxy." The antibody that was being attacked in her brain had not been discovered yet. So, the treatment was not cut and dry, and there would be some trial and error. He put together a plan, and we trusted him fully.

His lead researcher Trish met us the next day and asked us if we would be willing to allow the doctors to take samples of Grace's blood and bone marrow and follow her case for research so it could help others. We immediately said yes. We did not want anyone to have to go through what we went through, and if we could have one silver lining of the situation, we wanted it. We knew then that if we were ever on the other side of this, and if and when Grace was healthy again, we wanted to do something.

Since then, I have been able to speak to numerous parents around the country going through a similar situation. I do not have answers, but at least I have been in their shoes, and that is a comforting thing to be able to be a listening ear when you feel like no one else understands.

We established the Grace Fund for Autoimmune Research at UT Southwestern. The funds raised specifically go to Dr. Greenberg's research to hopefully discover more antibodies like the one that had not yet been discovered for Grace.

This was something that we had that was special and unique to us to help pay it forward.

Preserving What Matters

I once had a bride that also loved preservation and animals. She had 205 chickens and a few peacocks. The wedding schedule read like this:

- 4:55 p.m.: Sara Fay to wrangle the chickens back into their chicken coops
- 5:20 p.m.: Sara Fay to cue the albino peacock before the bride
- 5:30 p.m.: Sara Fay to cue the bride to walk down the aisle

You really could not make it up if you tried. I could not find the bride before the first dance. I found her back in the house in her bedroom, packing for her honeymoon. She said she had almost finished packing. I could not believe she was doing this now while all the guests were out in the tent on the dance floor. I said to her, "You go outside and do your first dance with your new husband and enjoy your friends! I will help you finish packing. You cannot miss your wedding!"

I glanced down at the suitcase, and all I could see was bright yellow. I took a step closer and peered into the rectangle rolling case and really could not believe what I saw. There were about fifty yellow rubber duckies in the suitcase. Like, the ones a baby would take a bath with. I looked at her with a curious glare and she said, "I have to take my friends with me on my honeymoon!"

I have some crazy stories and weird stories, but some weddings were just classic, timeless, and beautiful. Three of my favorite weddings reminisced on the past and used that to serve as the diving board for the design of the wedding.

One wedding in Bel Air was in the backyard of the bride's mother's home. We studied every design detail of the home: the paint color of the front door, the style of the furniture, every flower and tree that looked like it should naturally grow in the garden. You truly could not tell where the incredibly gorgeous home started and the tent began. It all flowed seamlessly. The bride was truly an old soul, and every detail of the day played off the beautifully restored home. In this case, a preserved home was all we needed for the wedding inspiration, and in turn, the wedding felt just like them.

Chapter Seven Takeaways and Reflections

Be proud of your past; be proud of where you came from. If you are not, then learn from that and uncover how you can make the future for your family and friends and community different. History does repeat itself and sometimes in the coolest ways, in fashion, in politics, in architecture, and in design. How can we reflect on the past and put our own creative spin on it to make it our own future?

Chapter Eight

RIGHT HERE IS PERFECT

True Happiness Comes from Being Fully Present in the Moment, Letting Go of Perfectionism, and Embracing Life as It Is Right Now

Busy is the enemy of peace. Busy takes us away from our purpose. Busy is not truly productive in the big picture. Busy means life's joys and surprises can't find a way into our lives because we're moving too fast to see and experience them. I don't know about you, but I don't want to move so fast that I miss my life.

—LARA CASEY

After years of striving, learning, and growing, I have come to realize that true happiness lies in being fully present in the moment.

I have realized that right where I am is perfect. At the time of writing this book, I am forty-two years old, and I finally feel like I have found deep happiness. While I have always been a happy and positive person, I am finally feeling peacefully happy. I have always been one of those people that is doing twenty things at once. I am the queen of multitasking. I never sit still. I rarely relax. I am always doing. I am always making lists. I am always answering emails or making calls. There is always something to do.

But what if I stop and enjoy the moment?

The past few years have taught me a lot about this. The biggest takeaway is that I try to be present in the moment and push the outside word and to-do lists aside. I relax and appreciate the small things in the moment.

Being present over perfect is a constant reminder and battle for me. Is it for you? Do you need that reminder? In the Instagram and Pinterest world that we live in, we are striving for perfection. It is in our face the second we start scrolling—the perfect dress, the perfect dinner, the perfect children that won again at the perfect sport. It's exhausting. To let yourself breathe, forget it all, and celebrate where you are in your life and who you are in your life—there is something freeing about that.

Try this for me. You should probably try this when you are alone and in a quiet place. Home alone is the perfect time with no judgment.

Are you ready? One, two, three … *scream!* Yes, do it—*scream*, as loud as you can. Do it again. Does it feel good? Are you laughing yet? I know you are smiling! Doesn't it feel good? Just let it all go, all the pressure, all the stress, all the need to be perfect.

Now look around where you are right this minute.

- What is beautiful about where you are?
  _____
  _____
  _____

- What are you thankful for about where you are?
  _____
  _____
  _____

- Name three small things about where you are physically right now that make you happy.
  _____
  _____
  _____

- Name three small things about where you are, not physically, but in your life, that make you happy.
  _____
  _____
  _____

    A while ago, I stumbled upon three questions that encouraged me to reflect on my current reality through the lens of gratitude each

the THROUGH *line*

year during this season. I hope they will be an encouragement to you as well!

- Where have you seen God at work this past year? Or what's one thing that you're grateful for?

  _____

  _____

  _____

- What is an unexpected blessing you've received in the past year? In other words, what is something that happened to you that wasn't what you wanted but has resulted in a surprising and unexpected blessing you couldn't foresee at the time?

  _____

  _____

  _____

- What do you want to be thankful for next year? In other words, what are you praying for?

  _____

  _____

  _____

Being in the Present

I realized that I was never present before. I was always in a meeting, but I was thinking about the not-so-great email I received five minutes before the meeting started and how I was going to respond to that to rectify that situation or angry client. The feeling of anxiety would build up inside me as I thought about how to respond to the situation and how to please that person. I could not focus on where I was and who I was talking to in that moment.

Have you ever felt that way?

I was always making lists in my head of all the things that I needed to do before I left the office that day. Then, how was I going to smile and get dinner on the table and the kids to bed and get back to answering those emails? Before bed, I would move all the things not done from my to-do list to the next day for a clean start.

Only it really wasn't a clean start because many of the things were not priorities. Most of these things would honestly not happen for months, but these lists hung over my head, making me feel like a failure even though I had done more in one day than most people do in a week!

Do you ever feel that way, feel like as much as you do in a day, it is never enough?

For me, there is always something to do.

Now I think back to that moment in Target with my kids, something I could never do when I was planning weddings because my phone would ring, or I would not be able to be present enough or would find myself getting upset and wanting to hurry.

Now living more in the present, I am so happy. My heart is so full. My hope for you is that you can learn from my mistakes, my hurry, my rush, my need for perfection. My hope for you is that it will not take you forty-two years to be totally present in the moment like it did with me.

This sounds very simple, but quit thinking, "What if?"

What if ...

... I hadn't quit that job to stay at home with the kids?

... I had taken action and started that side business?

... I had worked less and enjoyed the small moments with my family and friends more?

None of that matters. The time is now. The present is now. Enjoy the now.

Do that thing you've been thinking about doing. It is not too late. Do what makes you happy. If you are not sure how that thing is going to fit into your life, remember, you make the rules. You make it work for your life!

That was my same philosophy for weddings. A bride would say, "I actually hate cake; do I have to have a wedding cake?" The answer is no! You do you! If you hate cake, it probably does not make the best sense to spend part of your budget on a cake you won't eat and do not care about. If you are planning your wedding, prioritize what is important to you. If the traditional things do not feel right to you, then don't do them. Do something that feels like *you*! It is your wedding, your day, your life!

Is the Grass Always Greener?

You may daydream about the grass being greener, but would you have actually been happy if you chose the other route?

I have had the most incredible work experiences, experiences people dream about: weddings on the Amalfi Coast, work trips to Mexico, the Bahamas, the Cayman Islands, Jamaica, Italy, you name it. And it was fun! I would not change a thing about my career, weddings, travels, and the people I have met along the way.

I do wish I could go back and tell myself, "Relax. It will be OK."

I think the doer in me, the drive to never stop working, the drive to make every detail perfect, did in fact get me to where I am in my career. I would just hope that somehow my stories could help people know that it is OK to work. It is okay be a stay-at-home mom if you can do it. It is OK to do both. Growing up in an all-girls school, I was taught that I could do anything I put my mind to. It honestly never crossed my mind that I couldn't.

When I look back at the turning point days and decisions that got me to where I am today, I think the "not thinking and doing" is what made it happen. If I had sat there analyzing all the problems, things that I did not understand or know about the business, then I would have completely scared myself and talked myself out of it. I think especially today with social media, it is easy to get wrapped up in what people say about you. Everyone can see every picture, every post, what you are wearing, where you are going. There is too much on the table to be critiqued. I am thankful I went to high school and college pre-Facebook. I cannot imagine the pressure of the popularity counter with every like button. I think about this and how I can teach my daughter that she can do anything. It is an interesting question.

How can you teach your children that they can do anything? By your words? By your actions? The best example is them seeing you doing it!

> ## Lessons for My Kids
>
> - Never stop learning, ever. There is always something else you can learn.
>
> - You will make big mistakes. Learn from them, and get back up and keep going.
>
> - Learn the basics. Learn how to balance a checkbook, how to change a tire, how to drive a car, how to sew on a button, how to pay your taxes. Why do they not teach this in school?
>
> - Smile; it is going to be OK.
>
> - Always be honest, and always be true to your word.
>
> - Give love and you will receive love. Love people.

Now that you have heard my through line and what you can take away from it, it's time to discover your own.

Chapter Eight Takeaways and Reflections

What is your through line?

Your through line could be forming your own personal values; it could be tying your experiences together; it could be whatever you can weave the purpose of your life to be.

How can you tie all your stories together for good?

That is up to you.

It could be that every person's through line could be different, like our own thumbprint on the world!

Chapter Eight: Right Here Is Perfect

Our restaurant group's through line is completely different from another restaurant group's through line.

Big Life Event or Lesson

_____ Next life event/lesson

_____ Next life event/lesson

_____ Next life event/lesson

_____ Next life event/lesson

You have been given one life. If you feel like you are sitting here trying to figure it out, maybe you need to go back to the beginning. Write your response to the following:

- What makes you stand out?

_____
_____
_____
_____
_____

Conclusion

WHEN YOU GET DOWN, GET BACK UP!

I could write chapters and chapters of things that have happened to me at weddings and events.

Here's just a few examples I haven't even covered:

- A groom asked me for Viagra in his rehearsal dinner speech.
- A car was stolen from the valet at the wedding.
- I shared a bed with the bride-to-be on our first site visit.
- The father of the bride asked to borrow my debit card to tip vendors.
- The bride received a cease-and-desist letter from the groom at her wedding dress fitting.
- A florist passed out on drugs during an event install.
- I've been blackmailed, backstabbed, stolen from, sued, and sued again, and the list goes on and on.

I could have been on the sofa for the rest of my life eating potato chips and never gotten back up. I made a decision to keep going. I decided to not let any of these things get me down. Now, in the moment, yes I did. I cried, drank ranch waters, sang karaoke with my friends, and then I got back to work, got back to work in the business of being who I was, the business of trying to take the high road and not letting these situations tear me down.

So, wherever you are in your life, get back up! There is nothing better than proving someone wrong that doubted you or told you that you couldn't do it.

If someone tells me I cannot do something, my response is, watch me!

Now, I want to watch you! I feel like we have gone on a journey together through this book and through these life lessons.

Now go be present, hug the ones you love tight, laugh, and enjoy this beautiful life while it lasts.

As I lean back from the keyboard, I feel a sense of overwhelming joy for having had the chance to share these experiences with you and reeling in the importance of being present.

As I glance out the window and stare at my favorite oak tree, I notice a few deer grazing in the grass next to the pond. I am now choosing to close my laptop and enjoy this moment right here and right now. Because I know that my heart is full, and I know, in this moment, right here is perfect.

LET'S CONNECT!

Please visit our website at www.sarafayegan.com to get in touch and learn more about book signings, hospitality, and events.

Speaking Engagements

Sara Fay loves to connect with audiences in person. She specializes in a wide range of topics including:

- Finding happiness in the curveballs of life, family, and business
- Wedding- and event-planning
- Hospitality
- Balancing family and business
- Creating, building, and selling small businesses
- Leadership
- Creating a brand through line
- Home preservation
- Autoimmune research

Mentoring Sessions

Our mentoring sessions are perfect for young females who are interested in a dynamic career and need advice and actionable steps on where to start and how to get to where they want to be. Or for anyone who is shifting gears in their career or life and would like advice from someone experienced with navigating change. These include personal one-on-one Zoom sessions with Sara Fay as well as digital workbooks to help guide you through the journey.

Collaborate

We believe that all of our ideas and dreams are better together than apart. Reach out and let's see where a collaboration can take us!

The Grace Fund

Our daughter Grace was diagnosed with autoimmune encephalitis in November of 2021. Grace has what is called seronegative autoimmune encephalitis, which means we do not know which antibodies are attacking her brain cells. Her neurologist, Dr. Benjamin Greenberg, has an eloquent analogy to explain this. He says, "Think of the galaxy. We have names for about one hundred stars, but there are hundreds of thousands of stars in the galaxy that have not been discovered."

The Grace Fund aims to raise awareness and money for autoimmune research. An autoimmune disease is any disease that occurs when the body's natural defense system can't tell the difference between its own cells and foreign cells, causing the body to attack normal cells mistakenly. More than eighty types of autoimmune diseases exist and affect a wide range of body parts.

Let's Connect!

We hope that in the next five years, children showing symptoms like Grace will be more easily identified as having encephalitis, and these antibodies will help create cures and treatments. These cures and treatments will be for encephalitis and potentially other autoimmune diseases such as multiple sclerosis, type 1 diabetes, lupus, celiac disease, and rheumatoid arthritis.

TO LEARN MORE OR TO DONATE TO THE GRACE FUND PLEASE VISIT:

ABOUT THE AUTHOR

Sara Fay Egan is president and CEO of Beale Street Blues Company, a hospitality and restaurant group and entertainment company. Sara Fay, originally from Memphis, Tennessee, graduated from the School of Journalism and New Media at the University of Mississippi. After graduating, Sara Fay moved to Dallas, Texas, where she spent over nine years planning, designing, and executing weddings and events both locally and nationally as the national sales director and director of weddings for Todd Events.

Sara Fay opened Jackson Durham Floral and Event Design in 2012 and ran the company until she sold her ownership in 2019. At that time, she opened Sara Fay Egan Events, which specialized in planning a limited number of high-end destination weddings. Sara Fay has executed many successful weddings and events all over the world, including Texas; Oklahoma; Louisiana; Florida; South Carolina; Georgia; Tennessee; North Carolina; Maine; Washington, DC; Arizona; Colorado; Missouri; Nevada; New York; Oregon; West Virginia; California; Rhode Island; Michigan; Mexico; the Bahamas; Jamaica; and Italy.

Her understanding of all aspects of the hospitality industry has elevated her to a sought-after expert in the field. Her experiences in event planning, starting and owning businesses, and now running her family business—combined with her unbelievable personal and life experiences—compelled her to write this book.

But family is most important to Sara Fay. She and her husband, Merrick, have two children, Grace, thirteen, and Walker, ten, and she feels compelled to tell her stories and share lessons of family, life, and business.

www.ingramcontent.com/pod-product-compliance
Lightning Source LLC
Chambersburg PA
CBHW032046150426
43194CB00006B/437